LETTERS *of* GIACOMO PUCCINI

Giacomo Puccini

From a statue by Prince Paul Troubetzkoi
in the foyer of the Scala Theatre, Milan

LETTERS of
GIACOMO PUCCINI

*Mainly Connected with the
Composition and Production
of his Operas*

Edited by
GIUSEPPE ADAMI

*Translated from the Italian and
Edited for the English Edition by*
ENA MAKIN

NEW YORK
VIENNA HOUSE
1973

To my friends
Carlo Clausetti
and
Renzo Valcarenghi

Translator's Note

THESE letters were published in Italy in 1928 by Giacomo Puccini's friend and librettist, Giuseppe Adami. They are arranged in sections according to the opera to which they refer, and to each of the sections Signor Adami has prefixed an account of the inception and vicissitudes of the opera concerned.

The order of the letters in the Italian edition is not strictly chronological within the sections even when the letters are dated, while many which bear no date seem to have been placed with no particular regard to their sequence. In the present edition I have tried to arrange the letters chronologically within their sections wherever this could be done from internal or other evidence. Approximate dates supplied from such evidence are printed in square brackets. For the convenience of the reader I have headed the letters with the names of Puccini's correspondents, except in those sections which consist entirely of letters to Giuseppe Adami.

I have considered it useful to append footnotes on some points which the general reader may be grateful not to have to look up for himself, and on many others which would have been very difficult for the English reader to follow up at all.

To the quotations from Puccini's libretti I have for the most part supplied a fairly literal translation. In one or two instances of short tags, such as the *bravo giudice* of *Madama Butterfly* (Act II), I have used Messrs. Ricordi's version, as being more familiar to the English opera-goer, and therefore more readily recalling the scene which is indicated.

Among those friends who have helped me with suggestions, my thanks are due in particular to Signor Giuseppe Adami, who made clear to me many obscure points which perhaps only he could have explained.

E. M.

CONTENTS

Illustrations

LETTERS of
GIACOMO
PUCCINI

Introduction

FROM 1884—*Le Villi*—to 1924—*Turandot*. From the first definite step forward to the last glorious stage of his journey, it has been my desire to gather together in this book all that is most interesting in the letters of Giacomo Puccini. The popularity of his name throughout the world assures me that these letters will be of great interest, not only historically, but as throwing new and vivid lights upon the unforgettable figure of the great Master who is gone, and who was so much loved and yet so little or so imperfectly and superficially known. And I think that these letters can, better than any study or any biography, tell us what Giacomo Puccini really was.

When, [a few hours after his death in a foreign land, the city to which he had gone in search of life wished to pay him an immediate tribute of love and admiration, the few words that were spoken at the ceremony concluded thus: "Of the tears which you will shed for the musician many will certainly be for the man himself."]

It would have been impossible to sum up more simply the lofty secret of his art. The profound mystery, or rather, the essential reason, of his enormous popularity is revealed in this very real, yet almost indefinable, feeling by which we no longer distinguish between the man and the creator, no longer can tell if the tears which dim our eyes are our own or his, no longer know where success ends and immortality begins.

[Never has singer given himself more generously to his public, never has a more innumerable public stretched eager arms towards their singer. For the music of Puccini is woven of universal humanity, of limpid simplicity, of passion, torment, youth, and sorrow that cannot be spoken. His song is our

[15]

song, his thought our thought, his feeling our feeling, which, choked at times by the aridity of common things, leaps forth like a purifying flame from the spirit in the blessed hour of Poetry.

Few men, however, have any intimate knowledge of him, for there were very few to whom he revealed himself. His natural shyness often isolated him in long periods of contemplative solitude, which, with a sort of childish shame, he ascribed to his passion for shooting; and if anyone suggested how much better the society of men would be for him, he would extol some distant haunts of his down in the Maremma, with the woods and sea for company, and buried antiquities of Etruria, pale dawns, fiery sunsets, and vast silences in which there was no deception. Perhaps there alone did he succeed in dispelling his constant melancholy. But no one knew.

Many have had an entirely opposite conception of Giacomo Puccini. Too often it has been said that life showered her gifts upon him and fortune was easy—easy like his music, they said, flowing and sweet like his own inspiration. Fame had knocked at his door from the outset of his career, and through the door which Fame had opened Riches had entered. The fact that his works made their way, even where it seemed not only difficult but almost impossible to penetrate, had started, and indeed forged, the most solid links in a long chain of triumphs. And little by little, with the increase of his fame, grew the conviction that it was due to a certain mediocrity in his art, which pandered to the tastes of the public.

How often has one heard the phrase, "Puccini knows his public"! As if in the disparaging tone which coloured the words there was a disdainful reproach or a severe condemnation; as if this especial virtue of the artist were a tangible and vulnerable evidence of inferiority! As if Puccini never tormented his mind and his spirit, never searched the most intimate recesses of his feeling, never wrung his heart to cover his toilsome pages, but just tried his luck in an easy game, to amuse himself during the brief intervals of idleness allowed him by his innumerable other avocations!

One cannot say that many arose to defend Giacomo Puccini. On the contrary, those who should most have felt the duty of finding and pointing out the numerous reasons of the success which he was achieving were the strongest supporters of the stupid legend, juggling with a word, and willingly confounding *popularity* with *mediocrity*.

The man who had won the applause of the public of all nations—and he was an Italian—received his hymn of praise from the foreign critics, but from the Italians, with rare exceptions, he did not even gain recognition. In Italy *La Bohème* had been pronounced a failure, and *Butterfly* a work dead at birth. In Italy they would not admit—and there are some still who doubt it—that Giacomo Puccini came in a direct line after Verdi, with a solid, rich, definite, international personality, to create a new type of musical drama, which can today sustain any comparison, whose vitality is eternal, and whose intrinsic and technical value is everywhere acknowledged.

They would not admit the rich resourcefulness with which Puccini had combined in his operas right words, just proportions, and clear portrayal of characters and situations; nor, above all, that indescribable atmosphere which flowed from his music and which was the secret of its power to reach our hearts and remain forever unforgettable.

An easy success? No, a difficult one, assuredly. The public was conquered, but slowly and step by step, and the first performances were often received with an indifference which the critics confirmed. Since, however, there is only one art—that which arrives—and that which will never arrive is not art, Giacomo Puccini, although perhaps painfully, always arrived.

And so were formed the two main trends of opinion, that of the public, as opposed to that of the judges—the former exalting, the latter decrying—between which the sensitiveness of the artist was bruised and torn.

Now imagine the fine conscience of the artist placed between these two opposing judgments; consider that throughout his whole life he felt himself the subject of persistent attempts to disparage him, if not to destroy him utterly, and then tell me what enormous accumulation of vexations, disappointments, and discouragements make up the ceaseless torment of him who creates, and what titanic effort he must make in order to recover the sense of divine inspiration which from debasement will lift him to the stars.

It is precisely of this titanic effort, essential to the conquest of all his torment, all his doubts and disappointments, that Giacomo Puccini speaks to us in his letters.

For long years this torment included also the pain of poverty. *Le Villi* had already revealed his genius. But suddenly those who had called themselves his benefactors, and had helped him during his period of study at the Conservatorio of Milan, demanded the repayment of the money disbursed on his account, plus the accumulated interest of years. For at Lucca they were already talking of thousands and thousands of lire made by the young musician. The legend of Puccini was beginning.

What were his real circumstances at this period, however, he confided to his brother Michele, who died soon afterwards in South America, where he had gone as an emigrant and was working hard to make a living as a teacher of singing. To Giacomo his brother's position seemed so enviable that in April, 1890, he was writing to him in some such strain as this:

See that you at least make money! I have given up all hope of that. Here there are so few theatres, and the critics are making the public more and more difficult. I am terribly hard up. I don't know how I can go on. I am still getting the monthly allowance from Ricordi, but, of course, that is an advance. It isn't enough, and I am piling up debts. Presently, the crisis will come, and then God help me! If I could find a way of making money I'd come where you are. Is there any opening for me? I am ready, more than ready. . . . But the money for the journey? . . .

Fortunately, there never was any money for the journey, and the emigration of Puccini was never any more than a desire, often enough expressed in subsequent letters. In that one, for instance, in which he utters his anxiety about the production of *Edgar* at the Scala:

I am terribly afraid for the opera, because everybody is making a dead set against me. I am glad that you are making money! If you have any savings send them to me, and I'll put them away for you!!! [And here a row of exclamation marks indicates clearly where he was going to put them.]
I shall send you *Le Villi, Edgar,* and *I Crisantemi,* which is a quartet given with great success by Campanari at the Conservatorio and at Brescia. I wrote it in one night for the death of Amedeo of Savoy.

But even in the midst of his material difficulties, his enthusiasm for his work never deserted him. *Manon* was coming to life full of force and fire, and he was already thinking of a *Buddha*:

As soon as *Manon* is finished I shall begin *Buddha.* But it will be years before I can finish it. Meantime I am thinking about it.

It meant hunger, yet the artist set no limits to time. He took no account of his necessities in face of a future that was full of uncertainty. If he had the vision of a new work it was enough. It did not matter that it would take years to complete it. "Work! Work!" he wrote to me during the last years of his life. "There is no better prescription for reducing one's misery." It was the faith, never afterwards abandoned, of his early years, those years during which that prescription had to suffice even to make him forget the poor fare on which he had to live:

I worked till three o'clock this morning [at *Manon*]. . . . Then I had a bunch of onions for supper. . . . I am sick of this constant struggle with poverty!

And he was thinking of *Buddha*!

Manon Lescaut appeared and was a triumph. "*Manon*," he used to say, "is the only opera which has caused me no bitterness." It was with this opera, in fact, that he achieved fame. The public and critics were agreed about *Manon*. He now had to keep the height to which he had attained—keep it and climb higher. And then came *La Bohème*.

His disappointments began at once. Glory and riches? No! That was too much to allow to one who was so conspicuously climbing. His path must at least be sown with briars and thorns.

And briars and thorns they were—and generously strewn—which Giacomo Puccini, with firm step, avoided or trod down, his head high and his eyes fixed on the goal which shone in the light of his own sincerity. There came the overwhelming disappointment of *Butterfly*. It made no difference. On he went, fortified with faith and love and sacrifice, but with such thirst in his heart, such anxiety, such ardour to reach the heights, that they would suffice in themselves to crown with glory the silent torment of his noble spirit. His conviction was too firm, his will too steadfast, his approach to art too eager, for that lady of his desire not to open her arms to him. His creed had the simplicity of truth: "Only with emotion can one achieve a triumph that endures." They are his own words. "There are certain fixed laws in the theatre; to interest, to surprise, to move." These again are his own words. Let us not forget them.

Other words too his spirit uttered, painfully. Sometimes he was dismayed by the bitter difficulty of his work. Terrifying doubts would plunge him into desolate periods of inertia. Eager to miss no experiment which might in any way challenge the essentials of his own form of art or of his own personality, he followed, often anxiously, the so-called modernist movement in music, and sometimes he was terrified by it. Then he would be unable to resist any longer. He would run to any part of Europe at the announcement of an important event, if it was trumpeted by the supporters of the new school. He ran, watched, listened, and judged—but he returned reassured, always.

No, that was not doubt; that was not fear. It was something different. It was distrust of himself in relation to his own work, distrust which returned continually to torment him. "I am going to sleep," he would say, "so as not to torture myself with thinking." Or else, "I am sad and find no consolation." Or else, "Here there is sunshine and verdure, but in my heart blackness."

"I am a poor, unhappy man, discouraged, old, abject, nothing!" he wrote. "I don't quite say, *Muoio disperato*, but very nearly."

And again, speaking of his last opera: "I have finished the orchestration. The result is beautiful. Or is it possible that I am mistaken in thinking so?"

These doubts sometimes assumed agonizing proportions, when he thought that he had not given enough, had not given everything:

If the fever abates it ends by disappearing altogether. And without fever there is no creation. For emotional art is a kind of malady, an abnormal mental state, accompanied by over-excitation of every fibre and every atom of one's being.

And again:

I live in torment because I do not feel the throbbing life that is essential to the creation of a theatrical work which is to endure and hold.

And so on. As one turns over his letters one finds everywhere this pitiless scrutiny, this endless searching and craving, this continual fight against the dull and the lifeless. Then there were moments when he had the joyous assurance of having arrived, of holding solidly in his grasp the final solution which had appeared unattainable: "*Turandot* is getting on. I am on the highroad! . . ." Such occasional rays lightened the darkness. A few days after, the darkness would return: "I am in a devilishly bad mood," he would write, "I am utterly stranded. I cannot get clear. Let us hope that the melody which your lines invite will come to me yet, fresh and poignant."

But the torment of his musical creation was always preceded by the other, equally intense, which accompanied his patient and toilsome search for a libretto.

Before he could decide to write music to words written by anyone else it was essential that these words should lay hold of him and carry him along with them, firing his spirit as if they were his own creation, and destroying his last vestige of uncertainty. There were months and years of attempts which frequently resulted in nothing, and of hopes which wearied his spirit and aggravated the misery with which he beheld time pass while he composed nothing. There were projects which sprang up, matured, and were suddenly destroyed; convictions which seemed certain and which crumbled to nothing; visions which faded again before they began to materialise—leaving a greater void and a deeper darkness, where for a brief moment the tiny flame had flickered and shed a gleam of hope and possibility.

Then there were outbursts in which he gave vent to his feelings in vivid letters, throbbing with rebellion, and from which there always emerged, unmistakable, the figure of Puccini as a great theatrical artist, a genius born exclusively for the theatre. He wrote:

If I touch the piano my hands get covered with dust. My desk is piled up with letters—there isn't a trace of music. Music? Useless, if I have no libretto. I have the great weakness of being able to write only when my puppet executioners are moving on the scene.

And he added, with a bitter jest:

If only I could be a purely symphonic writer! I should then at least cheat time . . . and my public. . . . But that was not for *me*. I was born so many years ago. . . . And Almighty God touched me with His little finger and said: "Write for the theatre—mind, only for the theatre." And I have obeyed the supreme command. Had He marked me out for some other task, perhaps I should not be, as now, without material.

And he would plead that his librettists should

think of one who has the earth under his feet and feels the ground receding from him every hour and every day, as if a landslip would swallow him up.

If, however, even at these times of anguish, you asked him what was the object of his desires and aspirations and his eager searchings, what sort of libretto, in short, he wanted, he would answer in a phrase which was his maxim: "I want a libretto which can move the world!"

There is no doubt that anyone who saw him, as Renato Simoni has described him—

straight, tall, with shoulders squared and hat at a slight angle, his hands in his pockets, his step slightly swinging but strongly rhythmical, with his strong, sunburned face, his suggestion of rough shyness, and his good-nature—sometimes boyish and sometimes touched with compassion—

must have envied him—envied him as a conqueror to whom life had given everything and who had no longer anything to desire.

He, on the other hand, wrote to me a few months before his death:

I have always carried with me a great burden of melancholy. Perhaps it is wrong of me. But I am made so, and so also are made all men who have a heart and nerves: torment of spirit and eternal discontent!

It was that discontent with little things which to the sensitive temperament of an artist can be a source of more misery than great troubles; small shadows which thickened around him, but which the slightest ray would suffice momentarily to dispel. I remember the impression made on me by this passage in one of his letters:

Gui has written a fine article on Puccini in the review called *Il Pianoforte*. It is the first voice that I have heard raised to vindicate me, in the face of so many accusations and so many occasions when I have been forgotten or ignored.

The voice came from a publication which was almost unknown and read by a very small public. But to him it was enough for the moment that a few people could understand him.

Perhaps the one thing from which Giacomo Puccini derived unalloyed pleasure was his popularity—not, assuredly, for any petty personal vanity, but because it was to some extent a compensation for the bitter disparagement suffered from other quarters and because it was the world's recognition of his art and his work.

Especially when he was abroad he enjoyed it, and he liked the fun of describing it to his friends. Writing from Berlin, "They treat me here as if I were the Kaiser or the Crown Prince," and from Vienna, where the public almost worshipped him, "I have signed postcards for all the Fraülein Mitzi, Fritzi, and Schitzi, who munch pastries while they snivel over my music." And from London there was a joyful letter because the newspapers had called him "King of Melody." But the postscript was always the same: "I am longing to creep into my lair again."

He wrote in 1921:

Paris is beautiful, but it tires me. They are very kind to me everywhere. I had a wonderful reception last night from the public . . . including the *maîtres d'hôtel* at the Café de Paris. The little orchestra played *Butterfly*, and I had to get up and acknowledge it. [For one so shy as Puccini this was a great effort.] In every shop where I give my name they either ask for autographs or line up and bow to me as I go out. In short, we are popular, but old.

Here too one feels his longing to be back "among my pines."

Twenty-three years had come and gone and had made no difference to his feeling in this respect. This letter, in fact, is in perfect accord with another, written to a friend in Lucca as far back as 1898, the period of *La Bohème*, when Paris was beginning to take off its hat to the young Italian genius, and all the artists, from Zola to Daudet, from Sardou to Massenet, were doing him honour, not foreseeing, perhaps, that he would keep his place in the repertory of the French theatre with at least three performances a week. Anyone else in the circumstances would have enjoyed and savoured in full the greatness of the triumph, but not Giacomo Puccini.

I am sick of Paris! I am panting for the fragrant woods, for the free movement of my belly in wide trousers and no waistcoat; I pant after the wind that blows free and fragrant from the sea; I savour with wide nostrils its iodic, salty breath and stretch my lungs to breathe it! I hate pavements! I hate palaces! I hate capitals! I hate columns! I love the beautiful column of the poplar and the fir; I love the vault of shady glades; and I love, like a modern druid, to make my temple, my house, my studio therein! I love the blackbird, the blackcap, the woodpecker! I hate the horse, the cat, the sparrow of the eaves, the toy dog! I hate the steamer, the top-hat, and the dress-coat!

This free and contemplative life was always necessary to his inspiration, as was necessary also the melancholy which he loved, cultivated and cherished, but kept almost always jealously concealed.

If the adverse judgment of a critic or the bad execution of an opera could suffice for a moment to disturb him, success itself, on the other hand, had little power to affect him. He saw life rushing on and his eternally young spirit could not resign itself. No one would suppose that, after the triumphs decreed to *Manon Lescaut* in the unforgettable performances at the Scala in 1923, and after the enthusiastic demonstrations in his honour, Giacomo Puccini had enclosed in a few lines all his deep unhappiness. These lines, found after his death

in a bundle of jesting poems in which he used to play with
words and rhymes, and which he used to delight to send from
time to time to his friends, assume now a mournful and terrifying significance. What strange presage had seized him on
that desolate night? Why, while fame was ringing her loudest
peals about his head, was he calling upon death? . . . Un-
fathomable mystery! He was tired. He had walked too far.
He would fain have been far away in the infinite distances,
there to find the peace which life had denied him.

> When death shall come to find me
> I shall be glad to rest.
> For life is cruel and hard.
> Yet I seem fortunate to many!
> But my triumphs? They pass and leave
> So little! They are things of a day . . .
> Life runs on—toward the grave!
> It is the young who are happy!
> But who sees all this?
> Youth passes so swiftly,
> And soon the eye is searching—eternity!

Before releasing this book—as if seeking a justification for
myself—I read again, with pride and grief and infinite love, the
conclusion of a letter dated September 12, 1923: "Adamino,
better than anyone else in the world, knows his Giacomo
Puccini." These words especially are my justification for thinking myself not unworthy to gather together these letters of
the Master, choosing them from a very numerous collection
with tremulous and fervent care, conscious the while of communion with his spirit.

If I have sought to reveal to the reader some aspects of the
life, the glory, and the torment of Giacomo Puccini, it is that
I may see him honoured and feel him loved more and more.

I

Le Villi

IN ITS issue of June 8, 1884, *La Gazzetta musicale di Milano* displayed in large print, in the space usually occupied by the editorial article, the following announcement:

TITO DI GIOVANNI RICORDI
Music Publisher

in Milan, Rome, Naples, Florence, London, and Paris,
announces that he has acquired the sole
copyright, including rights of production and
translation in all countries, of the Opera

LE WILLIS

Words by FERDINANDO FONTANA
Music by GIACOMO PUCCINI

Produced with great success at the Teatro Dal Verme
in Milan

He has further commissioned SIGNOR PUCCINI *to compose a*
new opera with libretto by FERDINANDO FONTANA

This announcement, which marked the first step of the young composer towards his goal, served also as a culminating point in a family tradition of a hundred and seventy-two years. Indeed, Giacomo Puccini summed up in his own person five generations of musicians, of whom the first—like him, called Giacomo—was born at Lucca in 1712, studied at Bologna, and was appointed in 1739 musician to the republic of Lucca. He composed church and operatic music, and died at Lucca in 1781, survived by a son, Antonio.

Antonio Puccini, born in 1747, studied at Lucca, at first with his father and Matteo Lucchesi, then, like his father, at Bologna with Carretti. Returning to Lucca as organist to the *Serenissima Repubblica*, he died there in 1832 at the age of eighty-five, leaving a large number of sacred compositions.

His son, Domenico Puccini, born in 1771, studied first at Lucca and afterwards at Bologna and Naples. He was the first musician of the family to show more capacity for dramatic than for ecclesiastical music. He left, in fact, five operas, "produced with great success at that time." These were *Quinto Fabio*, *Il Ciarlatano*, *L'Ortolanella*, *Le Freccie d'amore*, and *La Capricciosa*. He died, only forty-four years old, in 1815.

His son Michele, the father of our Giacomo, born in 1812 and left an orphan at the age of three, was brought up by his grandfather Antonio. He studied, like all his predecessors, at Bologna, and then at Naples. He returned to Lucca as Professor and Director of the Musical Institute of the city. He was a composer of considerable taste and originality, and wrote a large number of sacred and secular compositions. Two *Masses*, one in G and the other in C, are esteemed as particularly beautiful. We have also by him an unfinished opera called *Antonio Foscarini* and a play entitled *Cattani*, or *La Rivoluzione degli straccioni*, which was produced with great success. At his death on January 23, 1864, he was honoured with a public funeral. The whole city shared in the mourning of his family, and the municipality settled an annual subsidy upon the widow, Albina Magi, deciding further to reserve his father's office of choirmaster and organist in San Martino for the little Giacomo, then five years old, and giving the office for the time being to his uncle, Fortunato Magi.

In consideration of the very straitened circumstances in which the Puccini family, consisting of a widow and seven little children, were left by the death of Michele, the position of teacher at the Collegio Ponziano was also earmarked for Giacomo. In the interval the post was held by the Abbot Nerici, an excellent musician, who handed over part of his salary to Puccini's widow.

Thus for Giacomo life did not open too joyfully. When the question arose of his entering the Conservatorio at Milan it was necessary to have recourse, in addition to the financial assistance of a great-uncle, Doctor Cerù, to a subsidy from Queen Margherita, who granted 1200 lire for one year. It is of this period of privations, of suffering, and of youthful ambition that the first letters in our collection treat.

Of the rapid progress of the young student, under the guidance of Ponchielli and Bazzini, from his *Capriccio Sinfonico*, the final composition submitted at the Conservatorio, to *Le Villi*, Puccini's first librettist, Ferdinando Fontana, wrote:

To leave the Conservatorio with the moral and material patent of *maestro* meant not to end but to begin a terrible struggle in that vast *conservatorio* which is the world. Giacomo

[29]

Puccini found himself a poor man, with a decided vocation for composing, but with the prospect of being forced, on pain of starvation, to renounce art for teaching. Nevertheless, he did not lose courage. The publishing house of Sonzogno had announced a competition for an opera, and he decided to try.

Ferdinando Fontana has described how Puccini got his first libretto:

It was in August of 1883. One fine morning when I had gone to Lecco, from Ghislanzoni's[1] retreat of Caprino Bergamasco, I fell in with the summer colony of artists from Maggianico. Among them were Ponchielli, Dominicesi, Saladino, and other distinguished men. Puccini also was there. We did not know each other well, but a strong current of sympathy had passed between us on those few occasions when we had met. I entered the same carriage as Ponchielli, who spoke to me of his pupil's intention of entering for the Sonzogno competition and suggested that I should write his libretto. There and then, with the memory fresh in my mind of the *Capriccio Sinfonico*, I felt the necessity of an imaginative subject for the young musician, and I outlined for him the story of *Le Villi*. He accepted it. The libretto was ready at the beginning of September, and the score was presented at the last minute. Puccini had had to send it in without making a fair copy.

As is well known, the committee did not award it the prize. But Arrigo Boito and Marco Sala, who at the instance of Fontana had taken the trouble to read the opera, undertook, along with a few others, to put together the few hundred lire necessary for the expense of copying and producing the work.

Le Villi appeared at the Teatro Dal Verme on the

[1] Antonio Ghislanzoni (1823-1893) was a poet and musician of Lecco, in Tuscany, librettist notably of *Aïda*.—TRANSLATOR.

evening of May 31, 1884, and was a success. Ricordi, the publisher, acquired the opera, and gave Giacomo Puccini a commission to write another at once. This was *Edgar*. During this period Giacomo's mother died. His triumph was darkened by grief, deep and unforgettable. He wrote to his elder sister:

I think of her continually, and last night I also dreamed of her. So today I am even sadder than usual. Whatever triumph art may bring me, I shall never be very happy without my darling mother. Be comforted as much as you can and take courage—the courage which so far I have not been able to find myself.

1

To Albina Magi

[*Milan*]
[*December, 1880*]

Dear Mother,[1]

So far I have no news of my admission to the Conservatorio, because the council meets on Saturday to consider the examinees and to decide whom they can admit; there are very few places. I have good hopes, having received the most marks. Tell my dear Maestro Angeloni that the examination was ridiculously easy. They made me harmonise a written bass of only one line, unfigured and very easy, and then they made me improvise on a melody in D major, and that was rather

[1] The first four letters were written during his early years in Milan to his mother at Lucca.—TRANSLATOR.

[31]

successful. In fact, it all went almost too well! . . . I go often to see Catalani, who is very kind. In the evening when I have money I go to the *café*, but there are very many evenings when I do not go, because a punch costs forty centesimi. However, I go to bed early. I get sick of walking backwards and forwards in the Galleria.[1] I have rather a nice little room, all clean and shining, with a fine seat of polished walnut, a real beauty.

So I enjoy staying in my room. I'm not starving. I can't say I live well, but I fill up with thick broth, thin broth, and thinner broth. The stomach is satisfied. It is a terrible day—sickening weather. I went to hear *L'Étoile du Nord*,[2] with Donadio singing, and Auber's *Fra Diavolo* with the famous tenor Naudin. But I didn't spend much. I got into the gallery for *The Star* for fourpence, and *Fra Diavolo* cost me nothing, because Francesconi, who used to be manager of the theatre at Lucca, gave me a ticket.

2

To Albina Magi

[*Milan*]
Thursday, 11 A.M. [*1881*]

Dearest Mother,

Yesterday I had my second lesson from Bazzini. It is going very well. That is the only lesson I have

---

[1] The monumental arcade which opens off the piazza of the Cathedral.—TRANSLATOR.
[2] By Meyerbeer.—TRANSLATOR.

so far, but on Friday I am beginning Æsthetics. I have
made myself this time-table: In the morning I get up at
half-past eight, and when I have a lesson I go to it. If I
have no lesson I practise the piano a little. I don't need
to do much, but I have to practise a bit. I am going to
buy a very good "Method" by Angeleri, the sort of
method from which one can learn a lot by oneself. I go
on till half-past ten; then I have lunch and go out. At
one I come home and work for a couple of hours preparing for Bazzini, then from three to five at the piano
again for some reading of classical music. I'd like to take
out a subscription for music, but I haven't enough money.
At the moment I am reading the *Mefistofele* of Boito,
which a friend of mine, Favara, from Palermo, has lent
me. At five I go to my frugal meal (special emphasis on
the frugal!), and I have Milanese broth, which, to tell
the truth, is very good. I have three plates of that, then
some other mess, a bit of Gorgonzola cheese, and half a
litre of wine. Then I light a cigar and go off to my usual
walk up and down in the Galleria. I am there till nine
o'clock and come home dead tired. I do a little counter-
point, but no playing; I am not allowed to play at night.
Then I get into bed and read seven or eight pages of a
novel. And that's my life! . . .

There is one thing that I should like, but I am afraid
to tell you, because I know that you have not money to
spend. But listen, it isn't much. I am longing to have
some beans—and they did cook me some one day, but I
couldn't eat them because of the oil, which is sesame or
linseed here!—and, well . . . I should like a little oil,

but fresh. . . . Do you think you could send me a "wee pickle"? A little is enough. I have promised to let the others in the house taste it too. And so, if my jeremiads bear fruit, will you be so very kind (how I am oiling you, talking of oil!) as to send me a little tin of it, which costs four lire, from Eugenio Ottolini, who has sent one to the tenor Papeschi. Here they are all writing operas as fast as they are able, but I do nothing. I am gnawing my hands with rage.

The other evening I went to hear the *Redemption* (an oratorio by Gounod), and found it very boring. Last night I went to Catalani's new opera.[1] For the most part, people are not going mad about it, but I think that from an artistic point of view it is very good, and if they do it again I shall go back to hear it. I am writing to you in the Dramatic Theory lesson, which I find very dull. I am dying to get home, because I have to compose a *Quartet* for strings for Bazzini. Tonight they are doing *Mignon* and Verdi's *Simon Boccanegra* (revised!).[2] The reserved seats cost fifty lire, and they are all gone already. What a rich city Milan is! Yesterday I went to Monza in the tram. . . .

The season ticket for the Scala is 130 lire during Carnival and Lent. Frightful, isn't it? To get a reserved seat it is 200 lire besides admission, which brings it up to 330. Isn't it appalling? Curse poverty! Yesterday I

[1] Alfredo Catalani (1854-1893), a native, like Giacomo Puccini, of Lucca. Composer of *Loreley* (1890) and *La Wally* (1892).—TRANSLATOR.

[2] Verdi's *Simon Boccanegra*, a failure at its first production in Venice in 1857, was revised in both words and music and produced with success early in 1881.—TRANSLATOR.

sneaked in for nothing to hear *Carmen*. It really is a beautiful work. What a crowd! Tonight I am going to eat beans at Marchi's.

3

To Albina Magi

Milan
August, 1883

Dear Mother,

I've been to Ponchielli's[1] and stayed four days. I had a talk with the poet Fontana, who is in summer quarters not far from Ponchielli, and he almost promised a libretto. In fact, he said that he liked my music. Then Ponchielli too intervened, and recommended me very warmly. It would be a good subject, which some one else has been considering, but which Fontana would like to give to me instead, and all the more as I really like it very much, there being ample scope in it for the descriptive, symphonic kind of music, which attracts me particularly because I think I ought to succeed in it.

In such a case I could enter for the Sonzogno competition. But, of course, Mummy dear, the whole thing is very uncertain. You see, the competition is open to all Italy, and not restricted and local, as I thought. Then the time is short. . . .

[1] Amilcare Ponchielli (1834-1886), composer of the opera *La Gioconda.*— TRANSLATOR.

I have not been again to visit Signora Lucca,[1] because she has gone to Bayreuth, where they are doing *Parsifal*, an opera of Wagner's.

I have a fortnight's board and lodging to pay, and if I come to Lucca I shall need twenty lire to redeem my watch and tie-pin, which are—enjoying the air of the mountain.[2]

Love and kisses.

4

To Albina Magi

Milan
May 13, 1884

Dear Mother,

As you will have heard, I am giving my little opera at the Dal Verme. I had not mentioned it to you because I was not sure. The expense of production is being shared by many gentlemen of Milan, and also some people of importance like A. Boito, Marco Sala, etc., who have pledged themselves each for a certain sum.[3] I have written to our relatives and to Cerù to help

---

[1] Of the Lucca family, the founders of the publishing house which became Ricordi and Company.—TRANSLATOR.

[2] *I.e.*, the "mountain of piety," *monte di pietà*, the Italian pawnshop.—TRANSLATOR.

[3] Here is the letter by which Ferdinando Fontana announced the subscription to his young collaborator:

My dear Giacomo,

I have today received sixty lire from a friend to whom I had applied for help, and who is joining us, along with certain also of his own friends. He wishes to meet you. I shall let you see the kind letter which he wrote. I was expecting at most twenty or thirty lire from him, instead of

me with the copies, because I shall need at least 200 lire
for them, perhaps even more.

How are you? I know that you will be just the same
as usual, poor little mother!

Michele[1] is well and sends his love. I shall write you
a longer letter soon. I have so much to do that I have no
time to write to my dear, kind mother.

Kisses.

5

To Giulio Ricordi

Lucca
June 19, 1884

Dear Signor Giulio,[2]

I have sent you the score and the parts of the
Capriccio Sinfonico. I sent the whole thing in accordance

---

which he has doubled it. That is hopeful. But I had already told you that,
as far as money was concerned, there w̶ ̶ ̶ no fear. Indeed, here is the sum
of ⋮ ⋯sent: Vimercati, L. 60; Marco Sala,
L. 50; Arrigo Boito, L. 50; the brothers Sala, L. 20; the "unknown lady" of
Marco Sala, L. 50: total, L. 230. There remain still Duke Litta, Noseda,
Count Sola, and Biraghi. Putting them down for at least L. 100, we shall
have L. 330. And Melzi? That will make it L. 430. As the expenses will
total L. 450 (250 for costumes and 200 for copies), you see that at the most
your contribution will be L. 20. At the moment, I am putting the finishing
touches to the libretto, and tomorrow I shall send it to Ricordi with a letter,
written in my best style. I shall arrange the *intermezzo* as you desire. Did you
receive the sketches for the scenery? Do you like them? You attend to your
music and do not bother about anything else. I assure you again that I make
myself responsible for it all.

F. FONTANA

[1] Puccini's younger brother.—TRANSLATOR.

[2] Giulio Ricordi (1840-1912) was for many years director of the house of
Ricordi and Co., of Milan.—TRANSLATOR.

[37]

with our arrangement that you should send it on to Turin. I should be glad if you would let me have the address of Maestro Faccio, because, as I am going to Turin on Monday or Tuesday, I could discuss the matter with him.

My mother is still the same, far from well, and, in fact, rather worse. You cannot imagine what a grief it is to me to have to be away from home. Well, we must hope for the best.

I should like very much to perform the *intermezzo* of *Le Villi* again. If you agree, the parts are ready, and all that is necessary is a certain amount of doubling of the strings. The orchestral parts of the opera are at my house at 13 Piazza Beccaria.

If your decision is favourable, you could send for them there.

Please give my regards to your wife and family, and believe me,

Yours sincerely . . .

6

Written by Puccini's Mother to Giulio Ricordi

Lucca
July 1, 1884

Dear Sir,

The money order for 200 lire has been delivered here, and as Giacomo is not in Lucca, but in Turin, I have addressed it to him there.

P.p. GIACOMO PUCCINI,
ALBINA MAGI, his mother

7

To Giulio Ricordi

[Turin]
[About December, 1884]

Dear Signor Giulio,[1]
We thank you very much for your most kind telegram. We had intended to write to you yesterday, as we had promised, but decided to wait till we were able to give you definite news.

There is no doubt that the performance of *Le Villi* at the Regio will be not only very far from what we wished, but also very inferior to that which it could have been in a first-class theatre.

The singers are a lot of old crocks. The orchestra is weak and lifeless, and even the baton of the valiant Bolzoni is powerless to infuse any spirit into it. What with being new to the orchestra, and because he is a little cold of temperament, he has not yet succeeded—and tonight is the full rehearsal—in making it go as Puccini wants it. I may add that Puccini, who is really very patient in his criticisms, does not dare to make any more, because the only suggestion which he made last night was received with scant courtesy.

The choruses are lamentably weak. At times they are simply not heard. And you know that the acoustic properties of the Regio are of the worst.

---

[1] This letter, signed by Puccini and Ferdinando Fontana, seems to refer to the production of *Le Villi* in two acts at the Teatro Regio, in Turin, on December 26, 1884, after Puccini's revision of it—*i.e.*, after the production at the Dal Verme in Milan.

I say nothing of the staging. We have not yet been allowed to see the scenery!

Puccini has little hope. I, on the other hand, believe in spite of everything that it will be a success. The first act is safe. The second will not in its beginning have the effect it should have, but the music is beautiful, and it will have more success as it goes on if the cast and orchestra learn anything from practice.

The less said about the ballet music the better. They have foisted a third-rate dancer on us as ballet master.

After tonight's rehearsal we shall send you further news. What troubles us more than anything else in all this is that we should in your eyes be cutting the same figure as all the rest of the miserable composers who, the stupider they are themselves, complain the more about everything and everybody. But you have asked for information and here it is, and perfectly true. And, besides, you know us, and we believe that you will not lump us with them . . .; especially as, notwithstanding the justifiable fears of Puccini, I, fortified by my own feeling and the admiring comments which everybody in the theatre is making about the work of the popular young musician, persist in believing that we shall have a great and real success, in spite of everything.

But at the Scala the preparations will have to be much more careful, because there they do things seriously. With the manager here, for instance, who refused to give Puccini even one extra instrument, it is possible to compromise, but at Milan it would be impossible.

Our greetings to you and Signor Tornaghi and regards to your family,

D. F. FONTANA

G. PUCCINI

8

To his Sister Dide

Milan
[1889]

Dear Dide,[1]

I have sent you the usual paper and enclosed with it some articles on *Le Villi* produced here again at the Dal Verme. Would you please let me know through Enrico—tactfully—what Franceschini arranged about that furniture—sofa, chairs, bed, etc.—which I handed over to him?

Love to you and Romelde, Otilia, Nitteti, and our nun. Do write to me sometimes.

I have had a series of requests for the repetition of *Le Villi,* and *Edgar*[2] is being given third in the Scala season.

Goodbye, kisses.

[1] This letter contains references to Puccini's other sisters, including the eldest, who was a nun in the convent of Vicopelago, near Lucca.—TRANSLATOR.

[2] This dates the letter as not much earlier than April, 1889, when *Edgar* was first produced at the Scala.—TRANSLATOR.

9

To his younger brother, Michele

Milan
April 30 [1890]

Dear Michele,[1]

Doctor Cerù has given me notice to pay him back the money which he spent on my maintenance as a student in Milan, with the interest to date. He says that I have made 40,000[2] lire on *Le Villi*! As my only reply I am sending him Ricordi's account of expenses, and he will see my share is only 6000 lire. What a difference! I should never have imagined it. The chemist is worrying me, and I shall have to pay your account of twenty-five lire. I am terribly hard up. I don't know how I can go on. I am still getting Ricordi's 300 lire a month but, of course, that is an advance. It is not enough, and I pile up debts every month. Soon the climax will come, and then God help me!

If I could find a way of making money I'd come where you are. Is there any opening for me? I'd leave everything and go. Don't forget to write to me, and write often. Tell me of everything that you are doing. Don't forget the house at Lucca. Nitteti[3] is left in great poverty, poor girl!

Tomorrow will be May Day, and I shall spend it in Switzerland, so as to be in the country. On Monday I

[1] Michele Puccini went to South America about 1889.—TRANSLATOR.
[2] £1600. The pound was at that time worth twenty-five lire.—TRANSLATOR.
[3] Her husband had just died.—TRANSLATOR.

dined with Erba. Bazzini, Martucci, Catalani and
Ricordi were there.

There is great excitement here about the first of May.
All the workmen are going on strike. As I have said,
however, I am going into the country.

Last night I worked till three in the morning, and then
I had a bundle of onions for supper. . . . If you have
any savings send me them—that I may put them away
for you! ! !

I shall send you under separate cover *Edgar* and *Le
Villi*, which Ricordi will give me.

Be wise and save as much as you can. See that you at
least make money. I have given up all hope of that.

Here there are so few theatres, and the critics are making the public more and more difficult. God help me!
I am ready, absolutely ready, if you write, to come. I'll
come and we'll manage somehow. However, I shall need
money for the journey, I warn you!

God bless you!

II

Edgar

AFTER the first production of *Edgar* at the Scala, on April 21, 1889, Giulio Ricordi summed up not only the events of the evening, but the judgment of the public and of the critics with nice impartiality:

The Milanese critics have attacked the libretto with great severity, and if they are more mild with the music, recognising the genius of the composer, they have nevertheless received it in such a manner that, if the artist in Puccini were made of less stern stuff, he would look for another occupation. But this severity on the part of the critics, who are sometimes so kind to mediocrities, must not at all discourage the young musician. On the contrary, such passionate and heated discussions, such long and numerous articles, more destructive than encouraging, are not written for mediocre compositions, which, although they may receive some praise, succumb, amid the indifference of the critics and the public, to their own lack of vitality.

The papers which acknowledged without reserve the musical value of the score were *Il Secolo, Il Pungolo,* and *Il Caffè. Il Corriere della Sera* was undecided, *La Lombardia* was violent and bitter, and *La Perseveranza* utterly annihilated both opera and composer. Yet the public had been unanimous in applauding the work. The report of the proceedings chronicled twenty-four calls and two encores in the first two performances, and three in the last, while "the season closed with an impressive demonstration of enthusiasm for Puccini, who appeared again and again, both with the cast and alone, in answer to the shouting and cheers of the entire audience."

But the opera, chiefly on account of the libretto, was never really successful, even after Puccini's attempts to improve it. To quote Giulio Ricordi again:

In *Edgar* there are such daring situations that it needed the whole force of the composer's genius to make them tolerable. Especially was the third act dangerous, with its tragic element of the funeral and the introduction of a catafalque upon the stage. It needed a powerful and inspired musician like Puccini to clothe with music the savage theme furnished him by the poet. But the very difficulties of this particular situation gave birth in the composer's mind to a passage of magnificent music.

Thirty-five years later, on December 3, 1924, at the funeral service of the composer in the cathedral of Milan, and amid the tears of a reverent crowd, this passage found its most winged expression, described by the *Corriere della Sera*:

Arturo Toscanini stood up to conduct the funeral elegy taken from Puccini's own *Edgar*, a passage suited to the occasion not only by the nature of the ceremony, but also for the words given to the singers, which Toscanini had, however, altered slightly to give them a more mystical character.

As the voices of the instruments rose in the cathedral a thrill of emotion passed through the crowd of listeners; it was the voice of the Master himself that they heard, in those fresh, youthful melodies which recalled one of the best moments of Puccini's inspiration: melodies which burst, impetuous and rich, from his heart, lofty flights in which the songs to come were already heralded.

When the voices of the soprano mingled with the sighing of the strings, the listeners felt as if in that moment the creatures of his operas were uttering too their last mournful farewell to their creator, as if their gentle figures were entering too into the temple to pray beside the flower-strewn bier.

From the altar of San Giovanni Bono the strains of the large orchestra resounded through the cathedral with a clarity that was marred by no echo, and with a volume of tone never before heard in our basilica. The grave elegiac mood and the delicate spring of Puccini's phrases had in Toscanini the perfect interpreter, who, under the influence of his emotion, gave to his rendering colour and expression worthy of the greatness of his art and of the sentiment which inspired him in that hour.

The critics—then—had nothing to say. Theirs only to be silent, to admire and to reverence. Puccini, companioned by his early melodies, was rising to immortality.

10

To Giulio Ricordi

Lucca
[1885 or 1886]

Dear Signor Giulio,

Fontana wrote to me the other day of your desire that I should come to Milan towards the beginning of next June. I am prepared to come; so, as far as I am concerned, the matter is settled.

But I should like to say something else, if my courage does not fail me. . . . As you know, my allowance[1] comes to an end in June. The opera is already far advanced. I received the libretto in May last year, and this Fontana will also corroborate, as he came to Lucca specially to finish it.

With your good judgment, you will understand that it is impossible in a year to complete a work of such importance as this and of such difficulty. At the climax of my hopes and my work I should find myself at a standstill, since I have no other means of subsistence and have, moreover, a brother to help.

Therefore I would beg of you to prolong the allowance, so that I may go on with my work free from worry. I should be grateful if you would write me a line to relieve my anxiety. Forgive this boring confession, dashed down, as best I could, in confidence. Meanwhile, I am pleased with my work, and dare to hope that you too will be satisfied. Send for me, then, when you want me. I shall come immediately.

Kind regards to all your family, and believe me,

Yours sincerely . . .

---

[1] He is referring to the monthly sum advanced to him by the firm of Ricordi while he was working on *Edgar*.

11

Written by F. Fontana to Signor Tornaghi

   Dear Signor Tornaghi,[1]

     As the end of the month is approaching, my friend Signor Puccini begs you to pay him in advance. . . .

Dots and repeat because you understand already. And my friend begs you also:

(1) To say to Signor Giulio that D'Ormeville (as a result of a certain visit made to Puccini here by Signora Mei and Signor Figner to hear the opera—and, by the way, Puccini likes Mei) has written to Puccini that he "must hasten the delivery of the opera because Signor Ricordi naturally does not wish to make the contract with the company until the completed opera is actually in his hands."

Now Puccini has worked like a slave, and within two months the opera will be delivered complete. He begs Signor Giulio therefore to have no fear on this account, and to make the contract, as he will certainly not fail him.

(2) My friend Puccini also begs very earnestly that you send him at once some upright scoring paper of thirty lines and twenty-four lines. This is urgent.

(3) He begs also that with your accustomed kindness you will remember that at the beginning of last July he had to go to Milan to go through *Le Villi* with Maestro G. Gialdini *at the latter's special request.* . . . Such a

---

[1] Tornaghi was a member of Ricordi's staff at Milan.—Translator.

journey caused extra expense to the Puccinian purse, never at all well filled, as you know. And the possessor of the said unworthy purse would be infinitely grateful if you would add to the monthly 200 lire some figure sufficient to cover that extra expense.

To avoid mistakes in the post and other similar pests, I beg you—finally, at last!—to send all this as before to my usual address at Caprino Bergamasco.

With many thanks in anticipation from Puccini and myself, and regards to Signor Giulio, yourself, Signor Blanc, and all the others, I am,

Sincerely yours,

FERDINANDO FONTANA

CAPRINO BERGAMASCO
August 22, 1887

12

To his Sister Nitteti

Milan

December 11 [*1888*]

Dear Nitteti,

I had the news of the birth of your baby. We are very glad. When you are able write and tell me about yourself. We are well.

As you may know, I have a performance at Turin on the 24th, and I go to the Scala about the 20th of January.

Let us hope that everything will go well. I am very

[49]

much afraid. I shall send you a paper immediately after. Michele is working hard at his studies, and I am pleased.

Did you receive the portrait of our dear mother? If Romelde is still with you, or Tomaide, tell them to write to me, especially Romelde, who never writes. My greetings to Alberto. How pleased he must be! He says that the baby is so big that he looks like a prize-fighter. Well done!

We are hoping to take a run down to Lucca in the spring, and if so I'll come to see you, and will have the pleasure of seeing the baby too.

Love to all and a kiss to the baby.

Your affectionate brother . . .

13

To his Sister Dide

Turin
[1888]

Dear Dide,

This is a letter for everybody, to save time. I am at Turin, as you see. The rehearsals are going well. Orchestra very good, but singers a bit thin, especially the tenor.

The performance will be Wednesday or perhaps Thursday (Christmas). I shall wire the result to you, and leave you to pass on the news to the others.

I am going to the Scala in Milan about the 20th of January. I hope to have good singers. Michele is in Milan, and if I have money I'll send for him to come here. The impresario is treating me very well, giving me twenty-five lire a day. But I spend a lot. I am in one of the best hotels, but tomorrow I'm changing and going with Fontana, who arrived today, into a private house. I hope for a success in spite of the singers, because I have the advantage of a good orchestra as compared with the Dal Verme one.

Greetings to Romelde, Otilia, Cerù, Raffaello, Massimo, your Ghigo, the girls, and the children, and to Assunta, Carolo, Carignani and the rest. Tell the girls to write, like you, to the Teatro Regio.

14

To his Sister Tomaide

[Christmas, 1888]

Dear Tomina,

Health and prosperity! A Merry Christmas to you and all your household. On the eve of the greatest and most important event of my life (*Edgar*) think of your loving brother. . . .

15

To his Sister Dide

Saturday night, 2 A.M. [1889]

Dear Dide,

I saw Gigi[1] the other night, and he is very well. He came here to see me. I had written him a note, not knowing where he was, as there are three barracks for artillery.

I thought him a little unhappy and disappointed with the life and its extreme rigour. The first days of a new life are hard for everybody. Michele has arrived[2] and is well. I enclose the letter he sent me, to save me copying it.

Edgar will be produced about Carnival. *Le Villi* is being given at Brescia and Verona. I am almost certain of a performance of *Edgar* at Venice. At the moment there are questions of agreements with artists to be settled, but I think that everything will be all right.

As regards those few trifles of Raffaello's, please send them *to me*. I am hoping to put my affairs in order as soon as possible. I am working very hard just now. I want to finish an opera for this next season at the Scala. I am sure of getting it produced. And so that makes three seasons that I shall have appeared on the bills of the first theatre in Italy.

All my household are well. I am living reasonably well and am sufficiently tranquil and happy. I have many

---

[1] Luigi, another younger brother.—TRANSLATOR.
[2] Michele had gone to South America.—TRANSLATOR.

[52]

enemies here, but I hope to make them burst with envy and rage if God grants me long enough life.

Good-bye. Love to Enrico and all the rest, and Albina, Nitteti, and Romelde from

Yours . . .

16

To his Sister Nitteti

Turin
Monday

Dear Nitteti,

Thanks for your letter. The opera will be given on the 1st of February. I am pleased, and everybody here is enthusiastic about it. I hope for a good result. The singers are a bit thin; but there's always something!

I have sent you the libretto. Good-bye. Write to me often. I like your letters so much.

Lots of kisses.

17

To Franco Faccio

Milan
April 25, 1889

Dear Maestro,[1]

Allow me to express to you in a few spontaneous words which come from the heart, rather than with polite and carefully chosen phrases, all the gratitude which I feel for the quite fraternal solicitude of which, always united with the great resources of your musicianship, you have given me so many convincing proofs during the producing and conducting of my work.

I assure you that I recognise in such efficient artistic co-operation one of the strongest of the forces which made for the cordial reception I had from the public of Milan. Through whatever grievous or happy vicissitudes art and life may lead me in days to come, I shall never lose the grateful memory of your able collaboration, which has been so much to my advantage. Nor must my gratitude be less for those excellent artists whose ability was equalled only by the good-will with which they worked to interpret my music, and for the painstaking chorus, who studied and performed *Edgar* with an enthusiasm and vitality which were truly admirable. I leave it, then, to you to say all that you can to the elect company of

[1] A letter written to the conductor after the first performance of *Edgar* at the Scala, April 24, 1889.

[54]

musicians whose perfect and entirely exceptional performance impressed me so greatly.

To you in particular let me renew my expressions of esteem and unlimited gratitude, and believe me

Yours sincerely . . .

18

To his Brother Michele

Milan
December, 1889

Dear Michele,

This is a hurried note because the mail-boat sails from Genoa at two o'clock tomorrow, and I have just risen from an attack of the fashionable malady, influenza. Elvira has a temperature just now of 104°. I am a rag. However, I hope to go out in a day or two and be at the first night of *The Mastersingers* on the 26th, which I hope will be good!

After the present season, Faccio is going to Parma as director of the Conservatorio there in place of Bottesini, who has died. There is much talk of Marino Mancinelli in Faccio's place. I should be glad. Indeed, I think him the only man fit for that post.

I had your letter, and was pleased to hear that you had already found something to do. Go ahead!—with courage and, above all, with honesty!

As soon as *Edgar* is published I shall send you a copy, and *Le Villi* too.

Write me all the details of your life there and of how the others are doing.

I must stop because I am tired and am going to bed. Tonio is still waiting for that chocolate from his legendary uncle in America. He is a rogue if ever there was one! I have dressed him in white now, with a red plush cap. He is like a cardinal of the Ascari!

Love and kisses.

I made this envelope myself, I swear it! If you want the secret, wire me.

19

To his Brother Michele

Milan
January 5 [1890]

Dear Michele,

The Mastersingers at the Scala was very well done. Gobbi was specially good. But nobody goes. Everybody here has influenza, including Faccio and many of the orchestra and chorus. Last night Coronaro conducted with distinction. I am going to Venice tomorrow, to hear Garulli with a view to a performance of *Edgar* at the Fenice, about which I hope to come to terms. Carignani is there, taking the place of Usiglio. I hoped to be able to arrange with Ferrari for *Edgar* in America, but my opera is going on too late. He is sailing immediately, so he will not be able to hear it.

I am working at *Manon*, and then I shall do *Buddha*.

But it will be some years before I succeed in finishing it. Meanwhile I am thinking about it.

In this coming year Cattaneo wishes to sing in *Edgar* at the San Carlo, where she is engaged. What do you think? Would you give her it? I fear and tremble and don't know what to do.

My feet are cold.

Brentano the architect has died, the one who designed the façade of the Cathedral. Poor fellow!

The girls are all well. Try to make money and lots of it. When there's no more work to do here, I'll come there too.

It's horrible weather: mist and fine rain. Half Milan is down with influenza. I believe that they are closing the schools tomorrow.

Good-bye. Write! My regards to your friends and love to you.

20

To his Brother Michele

Milan
February 6 [*1890*]

Dear Michele,

I am in bed again, but keeping better. I have had fever and pains. It's my third attack of influenza. Things are going badly at the Scala. *The Mastersingers*, although praised by the critics, bored the Milanese audiences, and that in spite of its being very well done. *Simon*

Boccanegra, on the other hand, was a success. *Il Re d'Ys*[1] looks like falling through for the moment because the singers are deplorable. I was present at a rehearsal, but I assure you that I saw nothing in it at all.

De Negri will do *Edgar.* He has had a great success here. I am terribly afraid for the opera, because everybody is making a dead set against me. If you find work for me after *Edgar* I shall come—only it mustn't be in Buenos Aires, but in the interior, among the redskins.

I'll send you *Edgar, Le Villi,* and *I Crisantemi,* a quartet played by Campanari with great success at the Conservatorio and at Brescia. I composed it in one night for the death of Amedeo of Savoy. *Le Villi* went very well at Verona and at Brescia. I'll send you the papers which speak about me after *Edgar* at the Scala, and you send me some money! It doesn't matter about the exchange being so disastrous! ! !

I must stop for this time. I'm going under the clothes, because I'm cold with my arms out. It is snowing tonight.

See that you save. Try to live sparingly always, and do you, at least, make money. I have little hope here. And then remember that we are trying to buy back our poor house at Lucca.

Yours affectionately . . .

[1] By Édouard Lalo, produced at the Opéra-Comique in Paris in 1888.— TRANSLATOR.

21

To his Sister Tomaide

[*1890*]

Dear Tomaide,[1]
What you tell me of Alberto surprises me very much. I don't know anything about it and had heard nothing. I have had no letters at all on the subject. I am very sorry, and I am writing this very day to Nitteti. I wrote to her for New Year, but she did not answer.

Poor girl! How will she be left, I wonder? There really is bad luck in our family. I too have been unfortunate this year. I had great hopes of *Edgar*, and then we could not give it because the tenor fell ill. It meant a loss to me of about 2000 lire, and besides. . . . Well, we must put up with it!

I am working now at *Manon Lescaut*. I am getting on well with it. I have no more news of Michele.

My love to Romelde and Otilia, Enrico, Giulia, etc.

I see Gigi nearly every Sunday and often keep him with me to dinner. He is well, and getting fat. He is smartening up a bit, too.

Good-bye. Keep well and write often.

[1] This was written in answer to a letter announcing the death of Nitteti's husband, Alberto Marsili.—TRANSLATOR.

22

To his Sister Dide

Milan
April 23 [1890]

Dear Dide,

You cannot imagine how surprised and grieved I was by the sad news of Alberto. I wrote at once to Nitteti. She wrote yesterday telling me in what an unhappy plight she is left. Poor girl! And now what will she do? What grieves me so much is that I can't do anything to help her. This year I have had the disaster of *Edgar's* not being given, by which I lost about 2500 or 3000 lire—all sure money, on which I had counted and which I had partly spent in advance. I don't know whether I can go into the country this year, and for me that is a tremendous sacrifice, because it is impossible to work here in Milan in the excessive heat. And then to take away the country from me is to take away part of life.

It seems that *Edgar* will be given next autumn in Madrid. I am working feverishly to finish *Manon* soon. I am keeping well—in fact, very well.

Love to Enrico, Giulia, and Paolino. I saw Gigi on Sunday. He is well, and as brown as a Turk.

Good-bye. All good wishes to you and your household from your brother . . .

23

To his Brother Michele

Milan
April 24 [1890]

Dear Michele,
I received your long letter and newspapers.
I hear that you have been ill. Your delay in writing was
making me anxious. I was interested in all the descriptions and details in your letter. Here there is nothing new.
You know already that *Edgar* fell through, owing to the
illness of De Negri.

Alberto Marsili has died, and poor Nitteti (to whom
you will, of course, write) is left in great poverty. Poor
girl! If I were even able to help her! But in my present
state of poverty it is a miracle if I keep myself going.

Mascagni has won the first prize[1] in the Sonzogno competition. The second was won by Ferroni, of the Conservatorio, and the third by a certain Spinelli, of Rome.
Now, however, there remains the performance at the
Costanzi, and we shall see how they stand the test. Pizzi
and Bossi, of Como, are getting their operas, which failed
in the competition, produced at the Dal Verme in May.
We shall see. I'll give you all the news.

Gastaldon gave a performance of his *Mala Pasqua*
with Teodorini singing, and it was fairly successful. Van-
bianchi has gone to Pesaro, where he got Petrali's post.
Likewise, Bossi is no longer at Como, but has gone to the

---

[1] With *Cavalleria Rusticana*, first produced in 1890.—TRANSLATOR.

[61]

Conservatorio at Naples. The Scala had a great success with *Hamlet*.[1] Calvé was singing. She is wonderful.

There are concerts at the Scala just now, with Martucci conducting. I did not like him. Gigi Mancinelli was in Milan yesterday, and informed me that he would like to give *Edgar* in Madrid in the autumn. We shall see.

In September I am moving house and going outside the new Monforte Gate, to a house in the *piazzale*. They are putting me out of here for playing the piano at night. Now that they've given me notice I'm fairly going at it.

I don't know if I shall go into the country, because I am absolutely on the rocks. If you are doing well where you are I'd come too, if there were something for me to do. Write to me about this. I am sick of the eternal struggle with poverty! At the last concert at the Scala they played a symphonic poem by Bazzini.

Buffalo Bill has been here. I enjoyed the show. They are a company of North Americans with some Red Indians and buffaloes. They perform magnificent feats of shooting and give realistic presentations of scenes that have happened on the frontier. In eleven days they drew 120,000 lire!

Our beloved heat is beginning here!

Love from us all.

[1] By Thomas (1868).

24

To his Sister Nitteti

[*1891*]

Dear Nitteti,
You will have heard of the really colossal triumph of *Edgar*.[1] Seven encores and forty calls the first night, and, if they had been given, there would have been ten encores the second night. I am pleased. Write me when you are coming; I shall be at Lucca.
I want you to be at the performance.
Good-bye. Lots of kisses.

25

To Giulio Ricordi

Madrid
March 8, 1892

Dear Signor Giulio,
Thank you for the *finale* of Act III. We do not go on till about the 15th or perhaps Thursday of next week. The slowness with which we move is incredible. I am very much satisfied with the few rehearsals which we have had so far. Pasqua has come to terms, but her voice hasn't; it is incredibly tired. Tamagno is very good, but I know that he has imposed on the man-

[1] At Lucca. A. Fraccaroli in *La Vita di Giacomo Puccini* (Ricordi, 1925) records such a performance in 1891.—TRANSLATOR.

agement the condition that they give him two other performances if he does not sing the part of *Edgar*. I assure you that all these things put together have discouraged and tired me very much. Let us hope that everything will go well now. The choruses are just passable, as likewise the orchestra. They do no more than sound the notes, and that with so little vitality that they seem as if they were all playing and singing from under the stage!

Yesterday a paper called *La Correspondencia* fulminated against the libretto, and this is unlucky, as the said paper is very much read. The composer Serrano is waging a fierce crusade against me, and so also, they say, is Breton. There is always a fly in the ointment! Well, we can only hope and—let them do their worst! Thanks for the telegrams from Turin; I'd be very glad to hear details. Greetings to all your family and to Signor Tornaghi. To you every good wish from

Yours sincerely . . .

26

To his Sister Dide

Milan
March 6 [*1905*]

Dear Dide,

Thank you very much for your letter. I am keeping very well, but my temper is not so good, because I cannot find subjects, and being so idle kills me. I am going now to Torre, and I am going to set to work and cut down *Edgar*, completely recasting the last act and correcting the others. I shall take out the second act, so that it will be a three-act opera. I have no new photographs. When I have them taken I shall send them to you.

Love to Enrico and Giulia and all good wishes from your affectionate brother . . .

27

To Giulio Ricordi

Torre del Lago
March 14, 1905

Dear Signor Giulio,
                    Carignani will hand you the rest of *Edgar* and will tell you of the unremitting work which I have put in during this month. I think that the opera in its present form should go well.

Carignani has worked like a nigger and, I think, to good purpose. Will you authorise him to give the singers their parts? I have written about him to D'Ormeville. But a word from you to the aforesaid author of *Dolce voluttà*[1] will provide the lever. I hope to see you soon.

I wrote to Giacosa, but have had no reply. I want to compose a comic opera [*opera buffa*]. I should not take long to do it. Let's make this stupid public laugh if we can, and they'll certainly be grateful to us.

                    Affectionately yours . . .

[1] He is alluding to the famous *aria* of Marchetti's *Ruy Blas* of which the libretto was written by D'Ormeville.

III

Manon Lescaut

THE night of February 1, 1893, marked the first great
undisputed triumph of Giacomo Puccini. A reporter
in a Milan paper wrote:

A few moments ago Manon uttered her last indescribable,
heart-rending cry. The curtain has just fallen, and Puccini and
his interpreters have withdrawn again into the darkness of the
wings after facing the glare of the footlights in answer to the
wild shouts of an immense public, transported with enthusiasm.
The echo of the last notes of the orchestra, epilogue to a
drama of human suffering, has just died away, and I am here,
confused, stunned, and wondering, and, what is of more importance, profoundly moved: moved even to tears. And I am
not alone in this. The public has wept with me, and even the
Turin musical critics, known for their reserve and their cold-
ness, confess that they were moved, and tomorrow they will
say it themselves in their papers.

And, in fact, the "confessions" were candid and unre-
served. The *Gazzetta Piemontese* thus concluded its criticism:

The last words of Manon are a cry to heaven for forgive-
ness of her sins and recall in the orchestral accompaniment the
minuet theme in the second act, but so darkly touched with
tragedy as to be hardly recognisable. Manon is dying. Once
more the four bars of the introduction, in the same key,
return to recall the idea of the infinite; and the parenthesis is
closed and the opera finished. But the clamorous demonstra-

tions of the public are not so soon ended. The enthusiasm rises to a climax; they shout, they yell, they want Puccini.

The *Gazzetta del Popolo* declared that this opera

left the audience stunned and overcome by emotion, and they broke into unanimous and enthusiastic applause, as from a need to persuade themselves that it was not reality, but a piece of scenic fiction that they had witnessed.

And the article concluded, "Puccini has won the great and arduous fight."

The *Corriere della Sera* said:

Between *Edgar* and this *Manon*, Puccini has vaulted an abyss. *Edgar* can be said to have been a necessary preparation, all redundances, all flashes and indications; *Manon* is the work of the genius conscious of his own power, master of his art, a creator and perfecter of it. *Manon* can be ranked among the classical operas. Puccini's genius is truly Italian. His song is the song of our paganism, of our artistic sensualism. It caresses us and becomes part of us.

It was such a vindication as Puccini had dreamed of. After *Edgar*, on whose libretto he had wasted so much beautiful music, he took no more risks. He had learned to his cost that for the composition of a vital opera a good subject was necessary. *Manon* fascinated him. Therefore it mattered little to him that others before him had clothed in music the inconstant passion of the mistress of Des Grieux.

It remained now to construct from the rich elements of the romance a good, picturesque, stageable plot.

Marco Praga was the first to be interested; and Praga himself now tells us the true story of the beginnings of this collaboration, about which so many inexact accounts have been written:

It was either the spring or the autumn—I do not now remember which—of 1890. One evening soon after the production of my play *La Moglie ideale*, I had dropped in, as usual, to Savini's for a game, when Puccini entered and asked to speak to me. We went out together and took a turn in the Galleria. Suddenly, without any warning, he said, "You must write me a libretto." I confess that although the unexpected proposal took my breath away, the friendship and admiration which I felt for Puccini made my resistance rather weak. I had never written a libretto; I had never even thought of writing one. "That doesn't matter," said Puccini, "especially as you don't even need to be concerned about the choice of a subject: it is *Manon Lescaut*. You have a sure theatrical instinct; you know how to construct. If you refuse to write the poem"—for although I am the son of a poet, I had made it plain at the outset that I would not write the verses—"you may choose your own collaborator."

"For that matter," I replied, "I can find the poet at once." Indeed, Domenico Oliva, who had just then published a much-admired collection of poems and who was a very dear friend of mine, seemed to me to be best suited for the work, and I proposed him on the spot to Puccini, who agreed. Before leaving us, he recommended me to read Prévost's novel again, leaving Massenet's libretto of *Manon* strictly alone, so that I might not be influenced in my conception, and to dash down my plot as quickly as possible, always keeping in mind his intention of composing an *opéra comique*[1] in the classical sense of the term.

A few days later I had a second conversation with the composer and explained to him briefly how I should divide the

---

[1] I have throughout thought this the best translation for the Italian *opera comica* as used in these letters.—TRANSLATOR.

acts: (1) The meeting of Des Grieux and Manon; (2) the wretched house of the two lovers, with the interested protection of Lescaut, his treacherous trick, his blustering immorality, his cynical counsels; (3) Manon amid the luxury which Geronte provides, the intervention of Des Grieux, the attempted theft, their flight, surprise, and arrest; and lastly (4) the desert and the death of Manon. Puccini was delighted. I wrote the plot. I submitted it to Puccini and Giulio Ricordi, who approved it. Domenico Oliva, to whom I had spoken at the beginning, and who had enthusiastically agreed to collaborate, lost no time in writing the poem, and the libretto was soon complete. In the summer I went with Puccini and Oliva to Cernobbio, where the Ricordi family was spending the summer, and we read the poem. Paolo Tosti was present at the reading. The success of it was complete. Tosti said that he had never read a more beautiful or more effective libretto. It was just the *opéra comique* of which Puccini had dreamed.

Back in Milan we concluded our agreement and Puccini departed with his, or rather with our, manuscript. Things could not have been better. But such a pleasant state of affairs was of short duration. A few months after, the composer was no longer satisfied with the plot or with the division of the acts. He could no longer feel that it was an *opéra comique*. He wished to eliminate the second act, substituting the third for it, and for the third finding a striking and dramatic situation. As a dramatist I did not approve of the change. Neither did I from my own point of view feel like changing the structure of the libretto. I declined the task, and handed over the whole matter to Domenico Oliva with complete liberty to change it as he thought fit. Oliva adopted Puccini's ideas and completely recast the work. The second act disappeared. The Hâvre act took shape, with the roll-call of the courtesans and their embarkation. But things went no more smoothly now than before. Every moment Puccini desired alterations and transformations. Oliva ended by wearying of the whole affair, and came to me

[69]

to tell me that he could not go on with the work and that he too was now withdrawing his collaboration. It was then that Giacosa, acting for Ricordi, approached Luigi Illica, who consented to take up and continue our work.

From that moment I heard no more about the libretto of *Manon* and its vicissitudes.

Illica's task was neither short nor easy, for he had the added difficulty that Puccini had already set to music some scenes which had accordingly to be let alone. Illica ransacked the already existing manuscripts, and, with a patch here and a stitch there, he fitted the old versions into the new. In a short time the first and second acts were finished. About the third act, on the other hand, the discussions were long, laborious, and heated. Meanwhile Puccini, to save time, was calmly going on with the music for the fourth act. Giulio Ricordi ceased to tremble for the opera. "If in the music Manon dies," he said, "the opera must assuredly live."[1]

In God's good time even the third act arrived in port, or, rather, weighed anchor with sails spread towards the distant Americas.

But when all was finished and the question arose of mustering the ranks of *Manon's* authors and establishing the paternity of the libretto no one would appropriate it. Everyone said that it should be all or none, and it was decided that the authorship should remain anonymous.

But from that anonymous partnership there was to arise, not long after, that union of two great names which

---

[1] Ricordi meant that if Puccini once completed the music for the fourth act the existence of the opera was assured and the libretto would be no serious difficulty.—TRANSLATOR.

gave to Italian opera the three wonderful libretti of *La Bohème, Tosca,* and *Butterfly.*

Some years later Luigi Illica wrote thus to Giulio Ricordi: "The intervention of Giacosa in the famous question between Oliva, Praga, and myself concerning *Manon* was the pleasant beginning of the later collaboration which certainly nothing but death could have ended."

28

To Giulio Ricordi

Chiasso per Pizzameglio
July 19, 1889

Dear Signor Giulio,

The only person who inspires me with trust and to whom I can confide all that is passing through my mind is yourself, who have shown me by so many signs how well disposed you feel towards me and what unmerited faith you have in me.

I am tortured by doubt regarding Giacosa's libretto.[1] I fear that the subject is not suitable for me; I am afraid that I shall not succeed in writing the kind of music it should have. I wonder if you could find a way of suggesting to Giacosa, without hurting him, that he should leave it alone for the present? On my return from Germany I should go and spend a week or so with him, and

[1] Giacosa, at the request of Giulio Ricordi, had sketched a plot, with scene laid in Russia, for a libretto. From this period, therefore, dates the beginning of the collaboration of Giacosa, Illica, and Puccini.

we could then come to an understanding about it. We should look for, and certainly find, something more poetic, more pleasing, and less gloomy, and with a little more nobility of conception.

That Russia of his frightens me, and, to tell the truth, does not convince me!

I am sure that what I am writing will displease you very much, but—supposing I had to compose an opera which I did not *entirely feel?*

I should be damaging you as well as myself. The contract with Giacosa could still stand. We could just change the clause about delivery by November and postpone it to December or January. I have plenty to do. I have *Manon* in August!

I am sure that with Giacosa I could find the subject which I need and that we could work in complete agreement and to the satisfaction of us all.

With Giacosa there will certainly be no repetition of the Paolo Ferrari-Ponchielli affair. He is too amiable for that.

I trust to your goodwill. Write me a line, and if possible do not scold me as much as I deserve.

With kindest regards . . .

29

To his Sister Dide

[*Milan*]
[*About June, 1890*]

Dear Dide,

I was delighted to have your letter and Enrico's. I am keeping well and working hard. I have no direct news of Michele, but I hear from a friend who has returned from America that he is director (!) of a school (!) at Salta.

Gigi is well. I saw him a few days ago. Please tell Enrico to have that suitcase sent to me, and that I shall send him the cost of carriage at once. Let me know about it. At the beginning of July I am going into the country, to Switzerland, as usual, but not to the same place. I shall send you the address later, because I do not know where I shall go. I have two or three houses in view, and have not yet come to a decision about them.

During the coming winter I hope to produce *Edgar* in several places. I have various contracts under consideration, and among them the Madrid one, which is important.

I was really unfortunate last winter. That accursed tenor! Poor wretch, as if it were his fault that he fell ill! I am working at *Manon Lescaut*, but I am desperate about the libretto, which I have had to get done over again. Even now there isn't a poet to be found who can write a good poem!

[73]

Did you see what a success Mascagni had? He was here yesterday; in fact, he had dinner with me. Carignani is here, looking for engagements. Luporini too is here; Catalani is delighted with him. Galeotti is here as well, an officer with a rich wife. He goes about in a carriage and pair with servants in livery.

Is it true, as Michele writes, that Signor Giacomo Sardini is in America? Carignani says he heard that he was working as a cook.

Is Romelde keeping well? They tell me that Otilia is just the same. My love to them all. And how is poor Nitteti getting on? What about Cerù? I wrote to him about the business of paying back with interest my maintenance for that year at Milan. I told him that it was impossible just now. With the sort of luck I've had up to now, it is wonderful that I get along at all. He told me that I was an ungrateful fellow and that I had made 40,000 lire with *Le Villi*. I replied by sending him the accounts, which I procured from Ricordi, and my sum total was 6500 lire! Imagine! What a difference! I have heard nothing from him since. Could you find out—but very discreetly!—what he is saying about it?

I have toothache. I have bottled a quantity of strawberries and put nine pounds of cherries in spirit—all in one day.

Tomorrow I am crossing into Switzerland to fix on a house, and in the evening I have an appointment about the libretto and am dining with Ricordi.

Yesterday I had a whole lot of photographs taken for nothing. I'll send you some.

Write soon. My regards to Enrico, Carlino, Paolino, and to you much love from . . .

30

To Giulio Ricordi

> *Dear Signor Giulio,*
> I have thought it advisable to send you Oliva's manuscript, that you may read it and get an exact idea of the defects and contortions which it contains. There are some good things in it, but the quartet, to take one example, is hideous. I do not understand why Oliva has departed here from the original scenario, which was so clear. The first scene, between Geronte and Lescaut, is good, as also is the second with Manon, except for some shortening necessary when Lescaut goes to fetch the old man, who is hiding. I think those asides are too long. Then if you look at the manuscript you will find some notes of mine, when Lescaut is talking with Des Grieux. The idea is perfectly clear: "My dear fellow, there are so many ways of making money when one is intelligent: cards, beautiful women, more or less young, etc., etc." Instead, as you will see from the libretto, all that is made vague, long, and tortuous. Then look at my notes. I do not like that disappearance of Renato and Lescaut to prepare a meal, because it makes Renato play an odious part. However does he come to the point of leaving Manon at the mercy of the old man? Do you remember how we fought with Leoncavallo to avoid that?

And now for the quartet, although there are many other weak points. How charming, logical and interesting was the quartet in the first sketch! That *mythological* entry of Geronte, then Lescaut's *war in Poland* to distract Des Grieux! That storm between Geronte and Manon! Then it was better that they should sit down at the table, as was decided. Where has it disappeared to, the little scene which fitted in so well, of the four drinking each other's health? In short, the whole scene of the quartet at table, which was rapid and full of interest, is replaced by another version of preternatural length and rhetorical wordiness, to the detriment of the clearness and rapidity with which the play should unfold itself. After the exit of Geronte it is good. But the fact is that I am not in the least satisfied, and I believe that you will share my dissatisfaction. The departure from the scenario has been an improvement in some respects, but in many others it has been greatly for the worse.

I shall write to Oliva that the manuscript, with some criticisms of mine, is in your hands. I beg and beseech you to see him and explain the contents of this letter and say anything else that you think apposite on your own account.

Trusting in your goodwill, I remain,
Yours sincerely . . .

31

To Signor Blanc

>   *Torre del Lago*
>   *Wednesday, July 18, 1893*

Dear Blanc,[1]

I give you notice that I have bought a bicycle!—payable, however, by monthly instalments. You will have a visit from the manager of the firm of A. Schlegel, 36 Foro Bonaparte, whom will you please pay on my behalf seventy lire as the first instalment and fifty lire every month afterwards, and I shall pay it up completely at my return to Milan in October. I shall be grateful if you will do me this favor.

I am well and very busy. How are things going? I have engaged Sthele for Verona, as Carignani says that she is a very good Manon. For Lucca Bolcioni has engaged Mazzanti and Borelli; I do not know them. Tell me what they are like. He speaks very well of them, but I am not so sure. I wanted Daddi and Carbonetti.

I advise you to keep an eye on Bolcioni about the scenery, that we may not have a repetition of the horrors of the Trento performance.

Greetings to Signor Giulio and Signor Tornaghi. All good wishes. . . .[2]

---

[1] Blanc was a member of Ricordi's staff at Milan.—TRANSLATOR.

[2] For the period when Puccini was working at *Manon* there are no letters of any importance. Puccini was throughout in direct contact with his publisher. This explains the gap which exists between these early letters and those mentioning the first productions in New York and Paris—*i.e.*, between 1893 and 1907. The last letter in this chapter deals with the celebration at the Scala of the thirtieth anniversary of the triumphant opera.

32

To Tito Ricordi

New York
January 19, 1907

Dear Tito,[1]

New York is extraordinary! *Manon's* first night was almost beyond description! Enthusiastic reception by a theatre filled to overflowing. I had to take six calls from the manager's box after the first act! Extraordinary ovations—I've never seen anything like it. After the second act I took seven calls from the stage. After the third I didn't appear. I just remained in the manager's box, applauding the artist while the audience shouted and cheered. After the last act, more applause and another public ovation for me—four calls. Cavalieri was magnificent. I was really struck by her temperament, especially in the moments of spiritual exaltation and of emotion. Her voice sways the audience as I would not have believed possible, especially in her high notes. Caruso is the usual marvellous Des Grieux. Scotti very good. Orchestral playing full of life and colour.

Kindest regards to you and your father. . . .

[1] The son of Giulio Ricordi.

33

To Giulio Ricordi

Paris
Monday

Dear Signor Giulio,

It was a real and complete triumph—a unique performance. I think I have never before had so organic or so perfect an *ensemble* for *Manon*. Little Bori was exquisite, and her voice, which had seemed slightly crude and small, achieved such an expansion in the theatre as to be heard even over the full strength of the orchestra in the third act.

Of course, the Paris Press has poured out abuse, particularly Bruneau. They say that Massenet's publisher left the theatre after the first act.[1]

At the Opéra-Comique they are still giving *Tosca,* with Scotti and Farrar, who were engaged for one *gala* performance and are now giving eight repeats. Tonight is the second of *Manon*, with receipts, they say, better than the first night.

I leave within three or four days.

You will know that the agreement has been signed between me and the Metropolitan for my journey to New York and my stay there. The terms are the same as the last time with Conried.

I shall see you again soon, dear Signor Giulio. I shall

[1] Massenet's *Manon* was first produced in 1884.—TRANSLATOR.

have two or three days at Milan and then shut myself
up again for the *Fanciulla del West*.

Affectionately yours . . .

34

To Giuseppe Adami

[Vienna]
November 1 [1922] 10 P.M.

Dear Adamino,[1]

I arrived last night at 8.30. It is raining.
Dress rehearsal on the 3rd. First night on the 6th. Then
I'm going straight home, where I hope to find the lines
for the end of the first act.[2] It is all finished except for
those voice parts of the three masks and the father and
son, a matter of ten minutes or so. And, by the way,
could you do me a great favour? By this time the libretto
of *Manon* is the work of everybody and nobody. Manon's
aria in the fourth act, the one that they usually cut, repeats three or four words again and again: *Sola, perduta,
abbandonata, io la deserta donna*.[3] I feel that one ought
to replace these repetitions by some other suitable words.
They won't be more than a line, perhaps. You will do it
in five minutes. Please do this for me and tell Valcarenghi.

---

[1] Adami, to whom this letter was written when Puccini was in Vienna in
1922 for a performance of *Manon Lescaut*, wrote the libretto of *La Rondine*,
of *Il Tabarro*, and, in collaboration with Renato Simone, of *Turandot*. He is
the editor of the Italian edition of these letters.—TRANSLATOR.
[2] Of *Turandot*.
[3] "Alone, lost, abandoned, a forsaken woman I!"

I remember that in their time—distant enough now—these repetitions annoyed me excessively.

My affectionate greetings to you all.

I wonder if Mussolini will introduce a little order into our national economy! I hope so.

35

To Signori Valcarenghi and Clausetti

February 2, 1923

Dear Valcarenghi and Clausetti,[1]

Please accept my very warmest thanks for the splendid gift which it was your kind thought to give me on the occasion of the performance of the thirty-year-old *Manon.*

This gift represents for me not only a testimony of the kindly feelings of the house of Ricordi towards me, but of your friendship also, which is particularly dear to me.

With kindest regards . . .

[1] The principal directors of Ricordi and Company since the retirement of Tito Ricordi from the firm.—TRANSLATOR.

IV

La Bohème

A STRANGE presentiment, of which we find a trace in one of the letters here collected, was in the mind of Puccini when Ricordi decided to give the first performance of *La Bohème* at the Teatro Regio in Turin. The facts proved him right. Where now was the enthusiasm of the critics who had lifted their voices in praise of *Manon* as of a masterpiece? The public, however, was faithful to Puccini, and as just as the critics had been unjust. The success of *Bohème*, from that first night—February 1, 1896—rapidly became more and more assured and more enthusiastically acknowledged. But on the morrow, in the Turin papers, what thunderings, what solemn warnings, and what indignation!

In the *Stampa*, Carlo Bersezio could not forgive Puccini for "composing his music hurriedly and with very little labour of selection and polishing." He described the music of *La Bohème* as "music which can delight but rarely move." "Even the *finale* of the opera," he declared, "so intensely dramatic in situation, seems to me deficient in musical form and colour." And he concluded —God forgive him!—

La Bohème, even as it leaves little impression on the minds of the audience, will leave no great trace upon the history of our lyric theatre, and it will be well if the composer will return to the straight road of art, persuading himself that this has been a brief deviation.

Luigi Alberto Villani, in the *Gazzetta di Torino*, declared:

The music of *La Bohème* is real music, made for immediate pleasure—intuitive music. And it is precisely for this that we must praise and condemn it.

More violent was Berta in the *Gazzetta del Popolo*:

We wonder what could have started Puccini towards the degradation of this *Bohème*. The question is a bitter one, and we do not ask it without a pang, we who applauded and shall continue to applaud *Manon*, in which was revealed a composer who could combine masterly orchestration with a conception in keeping with the best spirit of Italy.

You are young and strong, Puccini; you have talent, culture, and imaginative ability such as few possess: you have today conceived the whim of forcing the public to applaud you where and when you will. That is all very well for once, but for once only. For the future, turn back to the great and difficult battles of art.

In reply, *La Bohème* began from that evening its triumphal tour of the world.

But what seems almost incredible to this day is that a libretto so fresh and simple, of such a limpid spontaneity as this, can ever have given so much trouble to its authors. These, as we know, were two. The one, quick and agile, and of rich imagination, rapidly creating and destroying pictures and scenes, sketched and accumulated his material, preoccupied only with what was obviously

[83]

and immediately picturesque; while the other penetrated slowly and cautiously into that dense thicket, separating bush from bush and discriminating between flower and flower with careful wisdom and measured elegance.

Only in a fusion of the qualities of these contrasting characters could a perfect result have been attained. And it was without doubt because he had divined this that Giulio Ricordi had had the idea of associating Illica's quick, impetuous power of creation with the controlling thoughtfulness of Giacosa.

Murger's immortal story was too rich in characters, episodes, and scenes to be easily condensed into a dramatic synthesis. Puccini, firm and immovable in his undefined vision of the work to be created, was never satisfied, and, not content with supervising the architecture of the picture, he was unremitting and almost tyrannical in his preoccupation with what, to all appearance, were the most minute particulars. "I too want to have my say," he had written firmly to his publisher, "and will accept nobody's dictation." He was right.

But all Giacosa's goodwill, in the midst of this writing and rewriting and constant preoccupation with beauty and form, was strained to the uttermost. In vain, Illica clamoured that the libretto, after all, is just a canvas on which music must paint the picture, while Giacosa, on the other hand, replied to Ricordi's maddening requests for haste that he desired nothing more than to please him, but that he was not and could not be a facile scribbler, and that good writing meant time and labour. Of this labour we find painful and revealing traces in the

poet's letters, which are the letters, none the less, of a
gentleman and an artist sure of his craft.

"I refuse to dash down anything that comes. To add
line to line with the object of reaching the end would
seem to me unworthy and dishonest." Sometimes he de-
clares that "it is a terrible undertaking to reduce to the
required proportions an act crammed full of events. I
work desperately hard, but on the one hand I have to
make clearness my aim, and on the other I must not make
the act longer than three hundred lines." It is limits like
these that terrify Giacosa: "Shall I succeed? The further
I advance the more arduous do the difficulties become."

Then in the background there is always the spectre of
the modifications that Puccini will suggest: "Will it ever
be finished, or shall we have to begin all over again?"
is the librettist's anguished question to the publisher.

I confess to you that of all this incessant rewriting, retouch-
ing, adding, correcting, taking away and sticking on again,
puffing it out on the right side to thin it down on the left, I
am sick to death. Curse the libretto! I have already done the
whole thing from start to finish three times over, and some of
it four or five times.

At this Giulio Ricordi relents and writes no more reproaches. He tries tactfully to sympathise with Giacosa
and to raise his spirits, and the poet replies:

You say that you can understand and sympathise with the
slowness of artistic creation. But the trouble is that the work
I am doing on this libretto is labour devoid of stimulus, and
inspired by no warmth from within me. Art has its hours of

pain and travail, but in recompense it has its hours of inspiration, when the hand is too slow for the thought.

This relentless struggle with material which was becoming more and more arid for him, tied as it was to the exigencies of music, paralysed him. The necessity of shaping his line to fit the rhythm of the music quenched his inspiration and enthusiasm. He says:

I cannot, for all my trying, come alive in it; I cannot deceive myself and create for myself that illusion of reality without which one can achieve nothing. I have wasted more paper on a few scenes of this libretto than on any of my own plays.

But his complaints are never directed at the others. He takes the blame to himself: "I do not know whether it is the fault of the subject or of myself. Perhaps it is both, and perhaps it is entirely mine." He is aware of the loss which Puccini, who awaits in utmost impatience the completion of the work, may suffer through his delay, and one fine day his generosity makes him decide on abandoning the task.

In these circumstances, unable to hope to complete the task in the short time allowed me, blaming only myself and my own inadequacy for this shameful capitulation, and bitterly grieved by the necessity, I have come to the heroic decision to withdraw from the enterprise.

His resignation, needless to say, was not accepted. His torment, unseen and unknown, was to go on still for months and months, to his despair and for our pleasure. Puccini was immovable. Even after the delivery of the fourth act, that last act that had been already rewritten from start to finish four times, he wrote imperturbably to Giulio Ricordi:

> You will have the copy of Act IV by you. Will you be so good as to open it at the point where they give Mimi the muff? Don't you think it rather poor at the moment of her death? Just an extra phrase, a word of affection to Rudolph, would be enough. . . . When this girl, for whom I have worked so hard, dies I should like her to leave the world less for herself and a little more for him who loved her.

The Christmas of 1895 was a very merry one in the house of Giacosa, a Christmas, we might say, of liberation. *La Bohème* was finished. As a reward and in celebration of the event an imposing cake adorned Giacosa's table. This sweetmeat, sequel to so much bitterness, was the gift of Giulio Ricordi, and on the same day Giacosa sent his thanks in lines accepting the gift as a prize of victory:

> Garland of Gargantua,
> Feast of Pantagruel, inspiring
> Sins of greed
> In all who feed
> At the Christmas board of Giacosa!
> If of our work as yet unknown
> The splendid crown you are,
> What lordly prize will the people pay
> To *Bohème* on the wondrous day
> When she stands revealed
> In shining array?
> What prize will the people pay?

And what was it? With all due respect to the Turin critics, the prize was—fame.

36

To Giulio Ricordi

Torre del Lago
July 13, 1894

Dear Signor Giulio,

I have delayed writing to you because I wished for time to reflect seriously on the things which I am now going to say to you. Since my return from Sicily and the conversations with Verga, instead of being enthusiastic about *La Lupa*, I confess that I am assailed by innumerable doubts which have made me decide to wait till the play is staged before I make up my mind to put it to music.

My reasons are the extreme rapidity of the dialogue, the antipathetic characters without a single *luminous*, pleasing figure standing out from the general gloom. I had hoped that Verga would give more prominence to the figure of Mara, but it was impossible, given the existing plot. I have been helped towards this decision also by remarks made in his most recent letters. I do not think that you will be displeased by this! I am only sorry about the time I have lost, but I shall make up for it by throwing myself with all my heart into *Bohème*. In fact, for the last two days I have been eagerly waiting to set to work at it, and beg you to speak seriously now to Illica about the Quartier Latin act, about most of which we have already come to a complete understanding.

The second act—Barrière d'Enfer[1]—does not please me much. I am annoyed by all these trifling episodes which have nothing at all to do with the action of the drama. We ought to find an entirely different situation, more effective both as drama and as comedy. Illica will find valuable material for this if he will read Murger's novel. To conclude, I am working hard, and I hope that Illica or somebody else will hurry up and finish this libretto to my satisfaction.

As regards *La Lupa*, it is better to await the judgment which the public will pronounce upon the play. In Sicily I picked up nothing musical, but I photographed types, peasants' cottages, etc., all of which I shall show you when it suits you. Meantime I have need of a letter from you, which will put my mind at rest and not condemn my change of mind, which I should like to call "late insight." But better late than never. Meanwhile, kindest regards to yourself and all your family.

37

To Giulio Ricordi

Torre del Lago
September 7, 1894

Dear Signor Giulio,
You will have seen Illica. At the moment I am waiting for Giacosa's cuts and revision. (This is abso-

---

[1] In the final form of the opera the Barrière d'Enfer is the scene of the third act.—TRANSLATOR.

lutely necessary both for the unity of the work and because, with the stamp of added thought upon it, the libretto acquires, etc., etc.)

As it is, there is no doubt about its being an original work! And such a one! The last act is most beautiful. So is that of the Quartier Latin, but very difficult. I have had the mountebank taken out. It will be necessary to eliminate other things. It would be a good thing if you would glance through it too, and rid it of certain extravagances which are really quite inessential. For example: "The horse is the king of animals," and "Rivers are wines made of water," and many other such lines which Illica loves like his own sons (if he had any). What must be shortened—and very much—is the second act, at the Barrière d'Enfer. All that stuff at the beginning is unnecessary, and we have agreed to cut it down, as also to shorten the rest, including the final quartet. This, in my opinion, is the weak act. Shall I be proved wrong? All the better! But the one which I think particularly successful is the last. The death of Mimi, with all that leads up to it, is very moving.

Kindest regards. I await the "Quartier Latin" revised, abridged, and corrected by intervention of the Giacosian Buddha.

38

To Giulio Ricordi

Dear Signor Giulio,
    On Tuesday at 10 A.M. I shall be in your office.

I am surprised and puzzled by Illica's irritation. When he came here we were perfectly agreed—and he knew about *La Lupa*—and he deplored that I was not getting on with *La Bohème*, while assuring me that he would always be ready to help me in everything. Now when I go back to him he chooses to give himself airs. If he says now that I've given him the slip whose fault is it? The important thing was to make the work what it must be—logical, concise, interesting and well balanced.

At present it is none of these things.

Must I blindly accept the fiat of Illica? I have my vision of *La Bohème*, but it includes the Quartier Latin act, as I said the last time I discussed the matter with Illica. It must have the scene with Musetta, *which was my idea*. I want the death to be as I have envisaged it, and I am sure then of producing an original and vital piece of work. As for the act at the Barrière, I am still of the same opinion that I do not like it. There is very little that is musical in it. Only the drama has movement, and that isn't much. I should have liked to introduce a more musical element. We must remember that there is plenty of drama in the other acts. In this one I wanted a canvas that would allow me to spread my colours a little more lyrically. . . .

I hope that Illica will cool down, and we shall get to work. But I too want to have my say when the necessity arises, and I shall accept nobody's dictation. Meantime, kindest regards, and in hopes of seeing you on Tuesday,

Yours affectionately . . .

39

To Giulio Ricordi

Torre del Lago
Sunday

Dear Signor Giulio,

Very many thanks for your beautiful copies. Your indications are good. We can always add others if necessary. I am delighted that your impression of the music is a good one. Of course you are right—you must hear it again—but let me know when you return from Schörech, and I shall come with some new things for you to hear.

Meantime I am going ahead. I have written to Giacosa urging the alterations which I want in the first act.

All success to the treatment; write to me *constantly*; do not leave me alone in the deadly slough of my life!

Yours affectionately . . .

40

To Giulio Ricordi

[*Val di Nievole*]
[*1895*]

Dear Signor Giulio,
        I am sending you a small quantity of beans
and two boxes of grapes. The beans are very special ones,
and must be cooked in this way:
        Put them on the fire in *cold* water, which should be a
moderate amount—neither too much nor too little. Boil
for two hours on a slow fire, and when they are cooked
there should be no more than three or four spoonfuls
of liquid. *Ergo*, be careful of the quantity of water.
        N.B. When you put them on to cook add four or five
leaves of sage, two or three heads of garlic, salt, and
pepper, and when they (the beans) are half cooked, add
a little oil to boil with them.
        Turn over and you will see something that has driven
me to desperation and must be attended to if I am not
soon to be a corpse!!!
        If you read carefully you will see what the poet
wanted—a *quartet sung simultaneously*—but he has
made the mistake of employing *different metres* for the
different toasts.
        Marcel, as you see, intervenes to cut short the dispute
about *precedence*. Rudolph encourages the idea, and
Schaunard gives the signal, beating three, so that they
may all begin *together*. Don't you think so? Therefore

the idea of making them sing one after another disappears; there would be no sense in it otherwise.

And now, what is to be done about the different metres and treatments?

41

To Giulio Ricordi

[*Val di Nievole*]
[*Summer, 1895*]

Dear Signor Giulio,

No, Act IV is not short, far from it! Yet brevity is a great merit, as Colline also says.[1] With regard to the connecting passage, if we cut the toast, what you propose does not appear to me at all right, because Schaunard says, "Give me the tankard,"[2] and Marcel gives him it. Then Schaunard's laughing repetition which you suggest, "Give me the goblet,"[3] seems to me superfluous and out of place, as the friends have just laid the cup down in preparation for the speech which is coming. Don't you agree?

I should like Illica to write two or three lines, short or long as he prefers, with which to close the incident of Schaunard's interrupted toast. Then Rudolph can begin: "Better some dancing than making of speeches; clear the stage for action," etc.

[1] These words—*Gran pregio la brevità*—are given to Rudolph in the existing version of Act I.—TRANSLATOR.

[2] "*Porgimi il nappo.*"

[3] "*Dammi il gotto.*"

I am glad that you liked the products of Val di Nievole, and thank you very much for your blessings on the Doge.[1]

At 1.30 P.M. today Elvira[2] and I are off to Florence, to hear *Tosca*,[3] which they are giving tonight.

The famous shooting expedition has been put off till the 26th. It is better so! Now that I have made a good start with my work I am going on with it. As for the *pp's* and *ff's* of the score, if I have overdone them it is because, *as Verdi says*, when one wants *piano* one puts *ppp*. However, the *ritenendi* and *rallentandi* must go into the pianoforte arrangement—only the very necessary ones, of course—but please put them in, because there are none.

I repeat that the best course is to send me the scores and a proof that I may *do it myself*. In that way I can be sure that everything is all right. I shall send it back to you immediately.

Here it pours all day, and my boredom is complete. I beg you to see that the ties are put in where they ought to be. It would, however, be well if I were there too, but that is impossible. I have work to do and cannot afford the time. However, before they are engraved, may I have a violin part sent here that I may see them?

Kindest regards from
Yours affectionately . . .

[1] Giulio Ricordi used frequently to address Puccini in his letters as "The Doge."
[2] His wife.—TRANSLATOR.
[3] *I.e.*, the play by Sardou.—TRANSLATOR.

42

To Giulio Ricordi

Dear Signor Giulio,

Illica has sent me the copy. But, to tell the truth, that solo of Schaunard, of which he has sent me a rough draft, is not to my liking at all. It is not worth the trouble of changing the old version merely to make him say foolish and pointless things, and, as I see that it would be an endless business, I am leaving things as they are and going ahead. I shall be very glad to make the cuts in Act II. Then, as Schaunard is losing his lines, it would be well to give him the largest share in the famous toast, of which Illica has sent me only a shortened version, and not the entirely new form which he had promised me and which I wanted. That toast *will be my death*! I don't know what to do about it. It is a serious matter unless I find some new idea instead. . . . I'll leave it blank, and they can speak it!!!

The arrangement of Act III for piano is almost finished. I do not know if I shall go to Torre del Lago when it is completed, as I said I should, because the Marchese Ginori[1] is shooting at Montecristo.

You will have the copy of Act IV by you. Will you be so good as to open it at the point where they give Mimi the muff? Just a glance will do. Don't you think it rather poor at the moment of her death? Just an extra phrase, a word of affection to Rudolph, would be enough. No

[1] At whose invitation Puccini used to enjoy an occasional day's shooting at Torre del Lago.—TRANSLATOR.

doubt it is a fancy of mine, but when this girl, for whom I have worked so hard, dies I should like her to leave the world less for herself and a little more for him who loved her.

Very many greetings from us all.

Yours affectionately . . .

43

To Giulio Ricordi

[*Summer, 1895*]

Dear Signor Giulio,
With mingled anxiety and joy I await Illica's alterations.

You will have noticed that at the end when they are giving the muff to Mimi, *Musetta tries to take it back.* Why, I wonder? I hope that this little incident was not intended, as it is so much out of place at the moment of death. The line must be corrected and some expression substituted which will be suitable to the circumstances. Of the toast I should have liked to retain the ideas of the first three, leaving out the last, which I do not like, and giving the others a different form.

We are working (there are two of us) with whole heart and soul. When I have finished I am taking two days' leave and going to my never sufficiently loved Torre del Lago.

I am writing to Ginori today, and if, as I hope, I finish on Saturday, I shall be off to terrorize the *palmipeds* of my adoration, which have long been panting for my murderous and infallible lead. Boom!

On Monday I shall be in harness again for Act IV. I am exceedingly pleased with the first scene,[1] which I kept for the last. I warn you that we shall need four bells. Matins are ringing from the Hospice of Ste Thérèse and the nuns are coming down to pray. *Ensemble*: xylophone, bells, carillon, trumpets, drums, cart-bells, crackings of whips, carts, donkeys, tinkling of glasses, a veritable arsenal.

All good wishes and in expectation of a *final* version from Illica and with greetings from us all, including Carignani,

Yours . . .

44

To Giulio Ricordi

    Dear Signor Giulio,

        As I have told you, Illica sent me a copy of the solo of Schaunard, a very poor thing—a mere piece of padding it seemed to me. Not wishing to insist on Schaunard's solo, although it had seemed to me desirable, and in order to cut matters short, I have sacrificed it and am keeping to the printed version, while observing the cuts in the duet. I have written to Illica to that effect. I have again called his attention to the toast, of which so far I have had only a revised version, but nothing new

[1] He is apparently referring to the first scene of the existing Act III at the Barrière d'Enfer.—TRANSLATOR.

has been proposed to me. It makes matters worse that in the various arrangements sent me up to the present by Illica, *Schaunard* is suppressed, Schaunard who ought to be the pivot and the head, the characteristic, dominant element, in the toast. Don't you think so? Then I want a revision of the moment when Mimi dies—*"Le mani—al caldo—e dormire."*[1] Before these words some little affectionate phrase is wanted, something that my poor head cannot find and cannot even suggest, but which the seething brain of the Piacentine[2] will discover, especially under the stimulus of the wish and the powerful co-operation of the lord of Barasso.[3]

Clausetti writes me that he has promised an article on *La Bohème* to the *Mattino*, and asks for other details and information about it, and even some *lines of the libretto.* Tell me what I should do. Clausetti is an excellent mouthpiece. I think that it would not be a bad thing to give him Musetta's lines beginning: *"Quando men vo soletta per la via."*[4] They are so pretty! Write at once and tell me what to do.

Be on the look-out for singers.

Turin—so I read—will be the first city. I am not too much pleased about that—(1) because the theatre is bad for sound; (2) *non bis in idem*; (3) too near Milan. Naples and Rome should be the first. Mugnone writes that they are treating with him for Palermo. Try to get him engaged where *Bohème* will be given.

---

[1] "My hands are warm, now; I shall sleep."
[2] Illica.—TRANSLATOR.
[3] Giulio Ricordi.—TRANSLATOR.
[4] "As through the streets I wander lonesomely."

I am not at all happy that it should be given for the first time at Turin, far from it!

Well! Kind regards to you and your household from us all.

Yours affectionately . . .

45

To Giulio Ricordi

Friday, August 9, 1895

Dear Signor Giulio,
Your letters are the only ray of sunshine in this tiresome holiday which I should prefer to call exile! It is good for my work, however, which is going well and not too slowly.

Nothing has yet come from Illica. You will know from Carignani that I have sent to the copying office for the last part of the waltz. I wish to revise it, as I dislike its too precipitate ending. An addition of two bars would make all the difference. The copying will, therefore, have to be interrupted. I shall keep it for a few days only.

I beg you to see that the expression marks are put into the score of the first act.

I met the Crown Prince, who spoke very kindly of *Manon*, which he had heard at Naples.

Now, here is a problem for you: On p. 8 of Act III at Rudolph's words, *"Mimì è tanto malata,"*[1] Mimi has, as an aside,

---

[1] The authorised English version has: "Mimi is so sickly, so ailing."

Che vuol dire? Morire !
 Ma insieme !¹

That *ma insieme* alone like that means nothing. Its only purpose is the rhyme, because it has no other reference to the accompanying lines—and I wish to change it. You, my best of poets, *mender of other's faults*, will find the solution and send it to me.

Kindest regards.

46

To Giulio Ricordi

 Dear Signor Giulio,

 Thank you for *Parsifal* and the proofs of the libretto. They are all right, but *che sgambetta*² must be changed to *che balbetta*³ in the chorus which comments on the arrival of Musetta and Alcindoro, because when the chorus sings Alcindoro has already been seated for some time. I have sent Act IV to Illica, and am now without a copy. Please send me another copy. I am working hard. When are you coming? Write.

¹ "What's he saying? Dying!
     But together! "
² "Kicking his legs."
³ "Stammering."

47

To Giulio Ricordi

Dear Signor Giulio,
Here is the passage which I have altered.
Carignani will be in Milan on Monday morning, and
will be able to go to the copying office and see to the
score without your having to be maddened by a visit to
that house of cacography.

For the boys please put the parts in their correct places
—*i.e.*, a bar earlier than they are written.

Can you help me about the toast? It cannot be sung
by all together, as it is in the libretto. It would be spirit-
less and commonplace. I have decided that we shall have
to change the preliminaries and introduce earlier the
brindiamo insieme, the *brindisi quartetto*, and the *uno,
due e tre* of Schaunard.

Then I think that after each separate toast some cries
of approval are necessary, some words from the Bo-
hemians—a bit of drama, in short, for without it the scene
is too lifeless and not at all natural.

The toast, then, must be arranged so as to be sung by
each separately, and some lively comments must be introduced after each one.

With regard to my coming to Milan, I am ready when
you need me, but let it be as late as possible, so as not to
interrupt my work.

I think it best to leave the choice of the artists to you.

Thank you for going to hear Brendari. O Musetta, where are you? "I am still *in mente Dei*," she replies!
Greetings from us all, and especially from
Yours affectionately . . .

48

To Giulio Ricordi

Dear Signor Giulio,
I have definitely decided to abolish the toast —after long and mature consideration! Here are my reasons:

I think it is useless to prolong the quartet scene so much, since it is created solely for effects of contrast, and does not help the action forward in the slightest degree. I am making the herring dinner and the dance afterwards as merry as possible; Musetta arrives when the revelry is at its height, and this is the point at which we were aiming. I know too, from experience, that it is a mistake to write fine academic music for the last act. Add to that the defect under which the toast is still suffering of being written in different metres (impossible for a quartet). And as I should have to compose for the toast of each separately, I should also have to change the preliminaries of which I wrote in my last letter to you.

This is how I think it should be done: Corrections should begin from the words, *Leva il tacco, posa il gotto, non far motto,* etc.; then Schaunard's reply when he resigns himself to sitting down, finally overcome by his friends' uncomplimentary remarks on his passion for making speeches. Rudolph suggests a dance, and the suggestion is joyfully accepted. That is how I see it, and I believe that it will be effective without any superfluous chattering. The progress, moreover, is thus more rapid towards what is the whole point of Act IV, the arrival of Mimi and her death.

That is my idea. Please tell me what you think of it.

Will you please suggest this to Illica? I am sure that he will make the connection very well, and that Rudolph's suggestion of dancing will come logically and naturally. When once I receive the scene thus adjusted from Illica I am confident that I can bring the whole matter to a successful conclusion, and make an act which will provide *quickly* a good close to the opera.

Always yours affectionately . . .

49

To Giulio Ricordi

Dear Signor Giulio,

They are happy days for me when your letters arrive. The last one, with its news of your speedy coming, was received with general rejoicing.

When you come you will find the full score, arrangement for piano and voice, and arrangement for piano alone.

Illica can be useful in making further cuts in Act IV, which still seems to me too long. To tell you the truth, I feel tired, and an act which moves more rapidly will be better for me, and, I think, also for the public.

It would be well, therefore, if Illica were to come too.

Let me know in good time when you are coming, because the post here is slow, and, moreover, I might be away, as I am expecting an invitation from Marchese Ginori,[1] which is taking longer to come than I like.

I am sick to death of this holiday, of this house, of this impossible place. My thoughts are continually in my beloved Torre del Lago! But I shall recoup my fortunes this year, I swear it!

I shall pass the time until your visit in looking forward to it joyfully, and in repolishing Act III and thinking of Act IV.

Elvira and Tonio are well and send kind regards.

In *greedy* anticipation of your visit, I am
Yours . . .

50
To Giulio Ricordi

Torre del Lago

Dear Signor Giulio,
I agree with your letter entirely, but there is a difficulty.

Am I to finish this act or not? Am I to finish it in Milan? Is my presence so necessary? I can put in the metronome indications here. You have only to send me

[1] To shoot at Torre del Lago.—TRANSLATOR.

a metronome by parcel post and a copy of all that is printed, and I will do it at once. I am doing no shooting at all. Only when Ginori comes for one of his rare visits I go out for half a day, and that is all. I hardly leave my table. I am orchestrating now, and in a day or two I shall send you some music. I am very well on with the composition and pleased with it. It has been rather troublesome, as I wanted it to be in some degree realistic and was anxious also to make all these little snatches slightly lyrical. And in this I have succeeded, for I wish there to be as much singing, as much *melody*, as possible.

The act is composed almost entirely of logical repetitions. The duet *Sono andati?*[1] and Colline's *Vecchia zimarra*[2] are almost the only exceptions. I think that I have found a good beginning for the duet and an effective climax.

To conclude, therefore, leave me here in peace to drink in this splendid sunshine and enjoy this enchanting countryside.

You speak of *Manon* at the Dal Verme. I think that Mendioros, although she is a trifle cold, would be an excellent Manon. This is an opinion justified by experience, as I had her at Lucca and Bologna. Moreover, I see that she is very much in public favour at present for her good Desdemona.

I am glad that Mugnone is at Naples if they do *Bohème*. I await the metronome.

Kindest greetings to all your household from us all.

[1] "Have they left us?"
[2] "Garment antique and rusty."

51

To Giulio Ricordi

> *Torre del Lago*
> *Tuesday Evening at 7*
> [*End of February, 1896*]

Dear Signor Giulio,

Thank you for the telegram from Turin and Naples. What a splendid reception at Turin! Twenty-four nights!

I agree with you, Tito, and Illica about the *finale* of Act II, but the remedy you propose does not seem to me what is wanted.

Your way, I think, provides a better solution scenically, but the effect is icy. Those few words sung by Alcindoro *solo* at the end of the act are a veritable cold douche.

We need something more clamorous, and from everybody, that the curtain may fall on an effective close. I suggest that we cut out the passing into the distance and the trumpet repeat, and close with a few additional bars in the orchestra, or else we could make a short scene with students, taking care, however, not to fall into an imitation of the end of *Manon*, Act I.

In short, some change is necessary, but the change which Illica has made will not do.

I should like also to lighten the middle of the act somewhat—all these things we can arrange at Milan after Palermo, *i.e.*, in May.

On Saturday I ought to leave Livorno at two, in order

to be at Palermo on Tuesday, but if the money does not arrive in time I cannot set out because I am on the rocks. To return to Act II, at Palermo I can try to cut out the trumpet repeat and add three or four bars for the orchestra, to give interest to the close.

Pro Florentia. My friend Landi's telegrams from Turin to the *Nazione*[1] have given the idea that *La Bohème* has had a very indifferent success. The atmosphere is, therefore, a little distrustful, and it would be well to take some measures about it.

Could you perhaps write to Giulio Piccini (Jarro) and to the Conte di Barga, of the *Fieramosca*,[2] whose real name is Sabardi? (These are people whom I think you know.) Could Illica see to the staging? Act II must be staged according to Tito's ideas; it would be a great mistake to trust Grafiosi. I do not wish to indulge in evil prognostications, but I think that the opera will not be so successful in Florence as in the other cities, and for me Florence is very important. Do see what you can do about it.

I shall not be able to go there, because I shall be at Palermo. At the most I could be there for the first night. If Tito were still in Italy it would be an excellent thing for him to go. I do not suggest that you should, because I know that you cannot.

But I urge you to look to Florence, where it will be necessary to take some measures to get our ship launched successfully.

[1] A Florentine daily paper.—TRANSLATOR.
[2] Another Florentine paper.—TRANSLATOR.

I am still awaiting a reply to my last letter.
Meantime, I send you kindest greetings.

52

To Signor Caselli

> *Paris*
> *Tuesday, May 10, 1898*

Dear Caselli,[1]
    I do not receive a letter from you every day,
and that is a pity. Are you abandoning me in this *mare
magnum?*
    I am sick of Paris! I am panting for the fragrant
woods, for the free movement of my belly in wide trousers and no waistcoat; I pant after the wind that blows
free and fragrant from the sea; I savour with wide nostrils its iodic salty breath and stretch my lungs to
breathe it!
    I hate pavements!
    I hate palaces!
    I hate capitals!
    I hate columns!
    I love the beautiful column of the poplar and the fir;
I love the vault of shady glades; and I love, like a modern druid, to make my temple, my house, my studio
therein! I love the green expanse of cool shelter in forest
old or young; I love the blackbird, the blackcap, the
woodpecker! I hate the horse, the cat, the house-sparrow,

---

[1] A very great friend of Puccini's, a druggist at Lucca.—TRANSLATOR.

and the toy dog! I hate the steamer, the top-hat, and the dress-coat!

They are giving *Bohème* here at the end of the month. Will you come? I hope so.

Yours affectionately . . .

53

To Giulio Ricordi

Paris
May 15, 1898

Dear Signor Giulio,

Thank you very much for your kind and always welcome letter, and for the money order for 2000 lire. The rehearsals are going very well. Guirodon is beginning to enter into her *rôle*. She will make a rather childish Mimi, perhaps too ingenuous, and not very dramatic, but I think that this new incarnation will not be too bad; she will have a *cachet* of her own.

Everything else is going well. Even the tenor is pulling himself together a bit. Bauvet (Marcel) is very good. Fuyère makes a first-rate Schaunard. What a pity that he has such a small part! The others are excellent. Ismardon (Colline) is the only one who is not putting his mind into his *rôle*. Yesterday, however, he had a dressing-down from Carré, which made him feel very small indeed. Now Luigini has fallen ill with gastro-enteritis. I hope that it won't last long. The rehearsals go with a slowness that is phenomenal. The orchestra has not yet begun to practise. I do not know when we shall be ready. Certainly not at the end of the month!

I am not very happy here. I should like to be away now for the sake of my work. I cannot work here. I am suffering too much nervous excitement, and have not the peace which is necessary to me. An invitation to dinner makes me ill for a week. I am made like that and cannot be changed at nearly forty years old. It is useless to insist: I wasn't born for a life of drawing-rooms and parties. What good does it do to expose myself to the risk of behaving like a cretin and an imbecile? I see that that is what I do, and it grieves me very much! But, I repeat, I am made so—and you know me, only you; Tito does not, and he constantly insists that I must make an effort to smarten up, but with me insistence on this point makes it all the worse!

I don't want to make comparisons, because it would be ridiculous, but Verdi has always pleased himself in these matters, and, in spite of that, has had not such a bad little career!

So far, God be thanked, I have had my full share of success, and that without having recourse to methods for which I am not suited. I am here for the sole purpose of seeing that my music is executed as it is written. Boldini is making a pastel portrait of me. It has been raining for days, it is cold, and I am not well; I often feel tremendously tired and discouraged and have frightful headaches.

I shall see Sardou in a few days and will settle definitely the question of that eternal Act I.[1]

I do not know if I told you that they have paid no attention to our figure-sketches and scenery. I must admit, however, that the costumes will be much better, more correct, and prettier, especially the women's.

As for the language, I am getting on a little better. I am making myself understood a little more than at first. I am, however, still the ignoramus that you know. Almost everywhere I have gone I have found people who know *Manon* well, and they tell me that they like it better than their own. This has pleased me very much. I close this long screed with sincere wishes to you and to Italy for the quiet that is essential to our welfare and the progress of art.[2]

Affectionate greetings . . .

54

To Giulio Ricordi

Paris
May 26, 1898

Dear Signor Giulio,

Luigini has recovered and is back—*laus Deo*, because with Messager it was a serious business. The orchestra is having its first practice today. What a time

---

[1] Of *Tosca*, adapted from Sardou's play.—TRANSLATOR.
[2] An allusion to the disturbances of 1898.

we have spent on the *mise en scène*! Their slowness is unnerving and killing me.

I am thinner, and my disgust with *La Bohème* is such that I am driven to despair when I try to infuse a little enthusiasm and a little Italian vitality into these supine and passive employees. I hope that I am now nearing the end of this *via crucis*.

Then, with Carré one can do nothing. He wants to do everything himself and he has staged the opera—very well, I admit—learning it as he went along, causing thereby an incredible waste of time for me. I can hardly bear to wait for the moment when I shall return to my quietness. How I long for it!

I beg you to send me *some funds at once*, for I am on the rocks. Money disappears in Paris with nothing to show for it! On Sunday we are going to see Sardou, I think, at Marly. I say "think" because we are waiting for a reply from Sardou, who is ill.

In hopes of seeing you soon, and with affectionate greetings. . . .

55

To Tito Ricordi

Lucca
September 3, 1914

Dear Tito,[1]

Passing through Lucca, I hear that they are giving *La Bohème* in a very short version. You will know that the projected *Loreley* with Toscanini conducting, fell through owing to the fear and dismay caused by the outbreak of war.

I am annoyed that they have put aside the commemoration of Catalani and instead are giving a *Bohème* with a local—*i.e.*, a most mediocre—orchestra and chorus.

I beg you not to give them the opera. You will do me a very real favour, for which I shall be grateful.

Yours affectionately . . .

[1] On his father's death in 1912, Tito Ricordi succeeded him as director of the firm.—TRANSLATOR.

V

Tosca

THE idea of deriving a libretto from Sardou's *Tosca* had already occurred to Puccini while he was working on *Manon*, after his first hearing of the play with Sarah Bernhardt in the title *rôle*. He spoke of it to Illica, but afterwards thought no more about it. It was only after *La Bohème* that his attention again fastened on *Tosca*. In the interval, however, Illica had entered into negotiations with Franchetti, who had fancied the plot for a libretto. All the skill of Illica and Giulio Ricordi was needed to rescue Tosca from Franchetti and bring her back to Puccini, who had at last decided to make music for her.

In this, as in the former collaboration of Puccini, Giacosa, and Illica, the negotiations and discussions were long and laborious. Sardou himself, to whom Puccini had appealed, took part in them, and it was only after months and months of altering and rewriting that the libretto assumed that final form in three acts which so pleased the great French dramatist that he declared that the play as presented by the two Italian librettists was perhaps better even than in its original construction.

Nevertheless, while the work was proceeding, Puccini, as always, exacted from his poets constant transformations, cuts, and substitution of lines. Especially was he concerned about certain long flights to which Illica in particular loved to abandon himself. And this is where Giacosa used to intervene as a restraining influence upon Illica, while Puccini himself, with the most pitiless decision, would sometimes concentrate into a few words the prolixities which marred some of his situations. In illustration of this, we may cite that scene in the last act in which Cavaradossi takes his leave of life. According to the original version of the libretto, the artist, condemned to die, would have had to sing a kind of *Latin Hymn*, so called because in it he passed in review his art, his country, his dreams, and his hopes, in a re-evocation which was too literary and stereotyped to be suited to the agony of the moment. Puccini, on the other hand, with his instinctive knowledge of human nature, could not allow that the lament of Cavaradossi should be for anything else than the beloved woman whom he would never see again. And the Latin Hymn was accordingly transformed into that completely satisfactory *muoio disperato* which was afterwards, with unforgettable effect, to reach the hearts of all who heard it.

The first performance of *Tosca*, on the evening of January 14, 1900, at the Costanzi in Rome, took place in an atmosphere which was very far from tranquil and happy. There was a certain amount of hostility towards Puccini and diffidence with regard to the opera. The newspaper accounts of the first night are represented point for point in the following telegram to the *Gazzetta Musicale*:

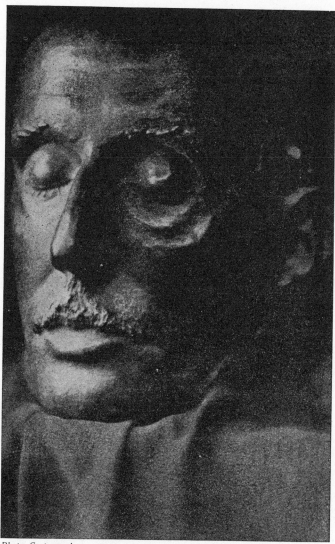

Photo Castagneri

The Death-mask of Puccini

Last night first performance of *Tosca*. Enormous crowd at theatre doors from 11 A.M. Orchestra hardly begun when stopped by shouting and stampeding of people unable to enter. Forced to drop curtain and begin again when silence restored. Act I: *Aria of Cavaradossi* (De Marchi), *Recondite armonie,* encored, two calls. *Te Deum finale* magnificent effect. Repeated. Wild enthusiasm. Five calls.

Act II: Torture scene, very moving. Tosca's prayer, *Vissi d'arte,* encored (Darclée). Four calls, end of act.

Act III completed the success. Scene of Cavaradossi's *E lucevan le stelle,* also closing duet of Tosca and Cavaradossi, encored. Ten calls end of opera, of which six clamorous for Puccini. Total, twenty-one calls, five encores.

Whole execution extremely nervous, partly from first-night excitement, partly from panic caused by letters sent to members of company threatening probable violence. These are the arts to which those jealous of the composer's fame vainly resort.

A rumour had indeed been spread, whether by chance or intention is unknown, that a bomb would be thrown in the theatre that night. The noise of the crowd which was struggling in vain for entrance was enough amid the general terror to cause the brief suspension at the beginning of the opera. Perhaps it was owing to this nervousness on the part of the public that, after the first night, *Tosca* was not judged in accordance with its real merit, and that the critics did not see in it another confirmation of the greatness of Puccini's art.

Puccini alone felt sure of himself and of his work. Indeed, to an unfavourable criticism of the third act, written to him by Giulio Ricordi, he had replied tranquilly but firmly, "This is not conceit on my part. It is the conviction of having expressed to the best of my ability the drama which was before me."

Once more Giacomo Puccini was right.

56

To Giulio Ricordi

Torre del Lago
July 3, 1896

Dear Signor Giulio,

I do not conceal from you that your refusal to give *La Bohème* again at the Pagliano in November has upset me very much, because I was very keen to have that season entirely devoted to my music.

There is in November at Florence, as at Venice, an International Art Exhibition, to which the King and Queen will come. It is a perfectly safe venture with no danger of poor returns, especially as the Pagliano will be the only theatre open, whereas in spring there is always the competition of the Politeama.

I believe that the clearest proof that an opera has been successful is its immediate repetition. As regards the production, since they promised me a very good one, we must insist that it be so both in its components and its general preparation. Mugnone, as you know, makes a real creation of my music, and it is certain that I shall never again have an opportunity of seeing both *Manon* and *Bohème* really well done in Florence. Therefore,

Signor Giulio, do not be inflexible, but give me the satisfaction which I so greatly desire.

With regard to *Bohème* arranged for small theatres, I leave it to you to do what you think best. The second act, however, will always be rather difficult scenically.

Busi writes me that she is negotiating for Fermo as Mimi. I believe that she is a good little artist. I have written telling her to apply to you. If you think her suitable, engage her.

At the moment I have no work to do. I am waiting for Giacosa to send me material on which to make a start.[1]

Kindest regards.

57

To Giulio Ricordi

Torre del Lago
November 4, 1896

My dear Signor Giulio,
Long life to Act II, carefully revised, polished, and speeded on its way by Puccini's blots. The third act will be really stupendous. At least, everything serves to make me hope so.

My health is excellent. No rheumatism, no fevers, no pains. But water everywhere, and I might say with Horace, *desinit in piscem*—or very nearly! Nevertheless I am very comfortable.

---

[1] He was waiting for the libretto of *Tosca*.

Very little shooting—but in a day or two I am returning to the Maremma to have a good spell of it.

My work is really getting under way. I am laying the
foundations with much care and, I hope, well. I shall be
in Milan at the end of November, and we shall then discuss matters to good purpose, as we usually do.

I have been to Florence, where I heard a good *Manon*.
On Saturday they are doing *La Bohème*. What a pity that
they have not been able to get Mugnone at the Scala! I
was present at a rehearsal, and I assure you that the performance was magnificent, with the sole exception of
Musetta, a girl called Castagnoli, who seems to me very
poor stuff. We shall see how she will turn out before the
public. Keep your eye on the bass Galli for Schaunard in
the Scala performance. He is very good.

Don't forget altogether about the performance of
Bohème in Rome.

Kindest regards. . . .

58.

To Giulio Ricordi

Dear Signor Giulio,
            I have read through Act II and have made
some changes which I consider necessary, as, for instance:
Come tu mi odii![1] is good, and *Tu mi odii?*[2] is impossible. Why has the last line been cut out: *E avanti a lui*

---

[1] "How you hate me!"
[2] "Do you hate me?"

tremava tutta Roma[1]*?* I put it in, and it serves my purpose. It is accordingly better to keep it.

With regard to the torture, do what you think best. I have not the music here, and I do not remember the notes. In substance, what you have written is all right. If that is how Sardou wants it, let us have it so. It makes no material change in the scene.

I am working, and I hope to dispense with the last triumphal effusion (the Latin Hymn). I think that I shall finish the duet with the words: *E mille ti dirò cose d'amor e gli occhi ti chinderò con mille baci.*[2] It makes a passionate close.

I have a bad piano, sent from Florence, and I have permission to work during the day, but not at night. Inclination? Yes, it is there, but it could be greater. Carignani has finished the arrangement of Act II and will send it off tomorrow.

Affectionate greetings.

59

To Giulio Ricordi

Torre del Lago

Dear Signor Giulio,

With what joy I await you I leave it to you to imagine! From Giacosa you will have received the oracle, with universal rejoicing.

[1] "And before him all Rome trembled."
[2] "And I shall say a thousand loving things to you and close your eyes with a thousand kisses."

Here the state of repose continues. Chastise me not! Malign me not! I have done *nothing—literally.* A sin confessed is half forgiven. I shall make up the time I have lost this winter. So no auditions of *Tosca,* no melodies. *Tutto tace,* as in *Fritz!*[1]

The weather is beautiful just now, and Torre del Lago is therefore at its most splendid. I shall receive you in my hovel, and you will pardon me if I cannot welcome you to the palace which you deserve and which I, as an emperor, should possess. We shall do our best. We are all very well. I am splendidly fit!

Tremendous enthusiasm at the concert at Lucca. Your *Fantasia Ungherese* was encored. I liked it very much. There was much enthusiasm also for *Edgar,* in which Sthele sang divinely and which was conducted by the nervous, but so entirely capable, Mugnone.

Many greetings from us all and in eager anticipation of your coming,

Yours . . .

[1] Mascagni's *L'Amico Fritz.*—TRANSLATOR.

60

To Giulio Ricordi

Monsagrati
July 31, 1898

Dear Signor Giulio,

Hot! Hot! Hot! You sleep by day and work by night! And here the night is really black—"I swear it, I swear it!" as Ferrani said.[1]

I am in a hideous, hateful place, drowned in the middle of woods and pine-trees so that one can see nothing, shut in by mountains, and lighted by a broiling sun with no breath of wind. The evenings, however, are delicious, and the nights enchanting.

I work till four in the morning from ten. The house and grounds are large, and indoors one is very comfortable. In fact, I am very happy to have fled to this tedious place where the human being is the exception. We are really alone.

I shall send on some material which I have already orchestrated, but I beg you not to look at it, as the calligraphy has deteriorated. I cannot understand it, but as I grow older I lose that neatness of hand which was so conspicuous a gift in me! Could you please send me on a bottle—not very large—of the usual Stephens' Blue-Black Ink?

[1] Manon Lescaut has these words—*"Lo giuro, lo giuro!"*—in her scene with Geronte and Des Grieux in Act II. Ferrani had sung the part of Manon.—TRANSLATOR.

I have heard nothing more of Illica. Can you give me his address?

I hope to stay here till October. (I say "I hope" because I do not know if I can stand it—not so much for myself as for my family, for whom this is a real sacrifice.) If so, I shall be able to get ahead with my opera, which I think is going more than well.

To you and to all, kindest regards.

61

To Signor Caselli

> [*Monsagrati*]
> 2 A.M., *August 18, 1898*

Dear Caselli,[1]

These butterflies may serve to give you the idea of the ephemeral character of human miseries.

As corpses let them remind you that when evening comes we must all die. While my brain is silently giving life and colour to my Roman heroine I act as executioner to these poor frail creatures. The Neronian instinct manifests and fulfils itself.

I send them to you to see if with your alchemy you can distil from them some new drug to add to the poisonous liquors which fill your den.

They will serve also as a remedy for the morning catalepsy which so assiduously pursues you. Ground and

---

[1] A facetious letter to his druggist friend at Lucca.

made into powder and sprinkled with calomel, they are efficacious against the heat.

Squeezed through a sieve and made into *purée* they are useful against the common evil of St Apollonia.[1] St Emidio used them against earthquakes. The ancient Greeks sucked them as lozenges and derived enormous advantages therefrom, especially against—hygiene! The French sit and suck them and enjoy a tickling sensation in the epigastrium while they are cured of elephantiasis.

In the eighteenth century they were used as a snuff excellent for scouring the noses of parish priests. Servants use them nowadays to scour copper.

Greetings.

62

To Giulio Ricordi

[Monsagrati]
August, 1898

My dear Signor Giulio,
I need these lines from either Illica or Giacosa in a metre precisely as indicated on the enclosed slip. They must be sure to keep the first four lines and the arrangement—Mario-Tosca—exactly as I have indicated. I beg you to see to it. You are more successful in obtaining what you ask, and you get it more quickly than I. Thank you so much.

[1] Toothache!—TRANSLATOR.

I need them soon, that I may send you the score; without them the duet remains incomplete.

I am sending you the alterations for Act IV.[1] They are clumsy lines, but they have the advantage at least of leaving the music unaltered and the *tu non mi scappi—dividi la parte*,[2] makes clearer Colline's intention of slipping away.

I am sending everything in great haste, because, since the receipt of your telegram this morning (26th), I understand your hurry. Please forgive me for not doing these till now.

Greetings to Tito and you all.

Affectionately yours . . .

63

To Don Pietro Panichelli[3]

[*Monsagrati*]
August, 1898

Dear Little Priest,

When you write to me it is always to give me news that I like. Tell our good and able friend Vessella from me what pleasure it gave me to hear of the effect produced by his arrangement of *Bohème*,[4] and thank him very much indeed.

I am working at *Tosca*, and sweating with the heat

[1] Of *Bohème*.—TRANSLATOR.
[2] These words were not eventually used in the libretto.—TRANSLATOR.
[3] A friend of Puccini's living at Rome.
[4] The arrangement for band by Alessandro Vessella.

and the difficulties which I encounter, but which will—
I hope—be overcome. Now I wish you to do me a kindness. At the end of the first act in the Church of S.
Andrea della Valle there is sung a solemn *Te Deum* of
rejoicing for a victory. Here is the scene: from the sacristy
enter the abbot in his mitre, the chapter, and all the rest,
while the people watch the procession on either side. In
the front of the stage one of the characters (the baritone)
soliloquises independently, or very nearly so, as to what
is happening in the background. Now, for the sake of
the phonic effect, I want some prayers recited during the
procession of the abbot and chapter. Whether it be by
the chapter or by the people, I need some murmuring of
prayers in subdued and natural voices, without intoning,
precisely as real prayers are said.

The *Ecce Sacerdos* is too imposing to be murmured. I
know that it is not usual to say or sing anything before
the solemn *Te Deum*, which is sung as soon as they reach
the High Altar, but I repeat (whether right or wrong)
that I should like to find *something to be murmured*
during the passage from the sacristy to the altar, either
by the chapter or the people; preferably by the latter,
because they are more numerous and therefore more
effective musically.

Look for the thing I need and send it to me at once,
and thus do a very kind deed to your sincere friend . . .

64

To Giulio Ricordi

Paris
Friday, January 13, 1899

Dear and beloved Don Giulio,

This morning I spent an hour with Sardou,
who told me of various things in the *finale* that he does
not like. He wants that poor woman dead at all costs!
Now that Deibler's[1] sun has set, the Magician insists on
being his successor. But I certainly cannot agree with
him. He accepts her access of madness, but would like
her to swoon and die like a fluttering bird. Then, in the
reprise[2] which Sarah will give on the 20th, Sardou has
introduced an enormous flag on the Castel Sant'Angelo
which, flying and flashing (so he says), will make a
magnificent effect; go in for the flag—he is keener about
that than about the play at the moment.

But I am still for the lament of Tito and for the end—
well, rather delicate and not too *éclatante*.

In sketching the panorama[3] for me Sardou wished the
course of the Tiber to pass between St Peter's and the
Castello!! I pointed out to him that the *flumen* flows
past on the other side, just under the Castello, and he, as
calm as a fish, answered, "Oh, that's nothing!"

[1] The French executioner.—TRANSLATOR.
[2] Of Sardou's play.—TRANSLATOR.
[3] This sketch made for Puccini by Sardou was thenceforth jealously treasured
by the composer.

Curious fellow, all life and fire and full of historico-topo-panoramic inexactitudes!

Well, the *reprise* was magnificent. Great enthusiasm over Act III with the encore of the whole quartet, an encore demanded with loud shouts, a strange and unprecedented occurrence here. Today I was at Tornielli's. He was very nice. Tomorrow I am dining with Carré and tonight with St Marceaux. Today I have been to lunch with Dreyfus, with whom I also dined yesterday. There I met Marcel Prévost, a very nice man. He is the first French artist I have met who speaks good Italian. Tonight is the second performance. I think that I shall be able to leave on Tuesday evening. On Tuesday morning I must go to see Sardou again—so the Magician has decreed. Perhaps he will insist on killing Spoletta too. We shall see.

It is not at all cold here, but rather like *scirocco* weather.

And now, dear Giulio, etc., etc. . . . .

65

To Giulio Ricordi

Torre del Lago
October 12, 1899

My dear Signor Giulio,

Your letter was an extraordinary surprise to me! ![1] I am still under the unpleasant impression. Nevertheless I am quite convinced that if you read the act through again you will change your opinion! This is not vanity on my part, no. It is the conviction of having coloured to the best of my ability the drama which was before me. You know how scrupulous I am in interpreting the situation or the words and all that is of importance before putting anything on paper. The detail of my having used a fragment of *Edgar* can be criticised by you and the few who are able to recognise it, and can be taken as a labour-saving device if you like. As it stands, if one rids oneself of the idea that it belongs to another work, if one wipes out *Edgar*, Act IV, it seems to me full of the poetry which emanates from the words. Oh, I am sure of this, and you will be convinced when you hear it in its place in the theatre. As for its being fragmentary, I wanted it so. It cannot be a uniform and tranquil situation such as one connects with other love duets. Tosca's thoughts continually return to the necessity of a well-acted fall on Mario's part and a natural

---

[1] Giulio Ricordi, having read the music of Act III of *Tosca*, wrote to Puccini a very long letter in which he said, with paternal solicitude but very clearly, that he did not like it.

bearing in face of the shooting-party. As for the end of the duet (the so-called Latin Hymn, of which I have not yet had the pleasure of seeing the poets' version), I too have my doubts about it, but I hope that it will go well on the stage.

The duet in Act III has all the time been the great stumbling block. The poets have not succeeded in saying anything good, and, above all, anything with feeling in it. (I am talking of the end.)

They are academic, academic all the time, and introduce all the usual amorous embroideries. I have had to contrive to get to the end without boring my audience too much and without indulging in any academics whatsoever.

Mugnone, to whom I have *sung* this act on several occasions, is enthusiastic about it. He prefers it, indeed, to Act IV of *Bohème*. Various friends and the members of my own household have formed an excellent impression of it. As far as my own experience of it goes, I am not displeased with it. I cannot really understand your unfavourable impression.

Before I set to work to do it again (and would there be time?) I shall take a run over to Milan and we shall discuss it together, *just we two alone*, with a piano and with the music in front of us, and if your unfavourable impression persists we shall try, like good friends, to find, as Scarpia says,[1] a way to save ourselves.

It is not, I repeat, conceit on my part. It is just my

[1] Scarpia to Tosca in Act II, *"Volete che cerchiamo . . . il modo di salvarlo?"* ("Shall we try to find the way to save him?")—TRANSLATOR.

defence of a work which is the fruit of my thought—and so much thought!

I never cease to encounter in my dear "papa Giulio" the signs of a great delicacy of feeling, not to speak of affection, which, you can be sure, is in full measure reciprocated. And I am grateful to you for the interest which you take and have always taken in me from the day when I had the good fortune first to encounter it. I disagree with you about this third act: it is the first time that we have had a difference. Therefore I hope, and go so far as to say that I am sure, that you will change your opinion. We shall see!

Toscanini is coming today—and perhaps I shall come back with him tomorrow or the day after. I shall wire to you.

I am still working at the prelude, which is giving me much trouble but which will come.

I shall have a very short time to stay at Milan, as I must get back to work and have to go to Florence on Sunday.

With all my affection, dear Signor Giulio, and very anxious to see you soon, I am,

Yours . . .

66

To Don Pietro Panichelli

December, 1899

Dear Panichelli,

Thank you for the information about the costume of the Swiss Guards and for your kind letter. Let us hope that *Tosca* will be successful and do honour to the composer. I hope that my friends in Rome, Vandini, Panichelli, and so on, will be pleased with the work of the vain *maestro*. Tell Vandini that the less *bataclan* they make about my person the more grateful shall I be.

After the sacramental three performances (if I am not hissed at the first) I am going into hiding in the woods which were a safe refuge for so long to Tiburzio and his companions. There I shall vent my sportsman's rage on the birds and compensate myself for the sufferings experienced during thirty or thirty-five days of rehearsals.

Yes, in the green rustic wilderness of the wonderful Maremma, where nice people go, I think I shall pass the best days of my life. But are you mad? To be out shooting—where there is really something to shoot—and after a success! It is the moment—the supreme moment—when the mind is really at peace! I want to make the most of it and I shall abandon myself to it. What do I want with banquets, receptions, and official visits?

I believe that my opera will have a performance *hors ligne*. Mugnone will put into the directing and conducting of it all the manifold resources of his artistic intelligence, and all the splendid executants, already inspired to do their best, will work wonders and *will give their all*. This time I am in good hands: management, orchestra, artists, and conductor. I have good hopes of a propitious Roman public and, above all, of a successful production of my opera. We shall see if my instinct is right.

Yours sincerely . . .

67

To his Sister Dide

> *London*
> *Sunday, 1 A.M.*
> *[May, 1900]*

Dear Dide,

I have just come from the dinner given in my honour by the Italian Ambassador. *Tosca* is being produced on the 12th. Last night *La Bohème* was given with great success at the same theatre, Covent Garden. I am going into the country tomorrow with Rothschild, who invited me last night.

I am well, but I have had enough of London. It is cold here; quite like autumn.

The rehearsals are going very well; with a rush, however, which savours of the American, and with no great attention to finish.

I was in Paris for two days on my way to London and saw the Fair. I shall go back there, but not for long.

London would be a better and more interesting place to stay in than Paris. It is the language difficulty which is so depressing.

I don't understand a syllable of it. Well, I know the numerals (the first ten) and some addresses to which I can go in a cab!

I am going to bed. It is late. I have written ten letters.

Your affectionate . . .

68

To Giulio Ricordi

Torre del Lago
August 16, 1900

My dear Signor Giulio,

I heard from Manolo, who came to see me after his visit to Montecatini, that your rheumatism was improving. By now I hope that you will have quite recovered. I am bored to death because I have no work to do. My lack of work has brought in its train an utter distaste for even letter-writing. I can never make up my mind to start. I have a mountain of them here on my desk to answer! I have begun today, however, with you. Well, I am nothing more nor less than an unemployed workman[1] of yours.

Neither from Illica nor from Giacosa have I any news, not even a single suggestion! So that I am truly and utterly forgotten.

[1] *Operaio:* a pun on the double sense of *opera* in Italian.—TRANSLATOR.

I should be grateful to hear from you whether you have written to New York for that American subject.[1] I am thinking of it continually. When I was in Paris I got some one to ask Zola again for *L'Abbé Mouret* and also if the report was true, which was published in the papers, that Leoncavallo had been given the exclusive right of that subject, but Zola replied, as he had replied to me the first time, that it was Massenet. Therefore, that subject too is out of the question. Must I come back to Marie Antoinette? If it were not for the already too old and thoroughly exploited subject of the Revolution!

I am eating my heart out in this inactivity. My best years (the last of my youth) are passing. It is a shame.

It is very comfortable here. No mosquitoes, thanks to the zinc screens in all the windows. The house is convenient and quiet.

If you want to give us a great treat, when you are better you should take a run over to see us. Come! You cannot imagine the pleasure it would give us. Write me news of yourself.

In a few days I am going to Lucca for the rehearsals of *Tosca*. I shall let you know what they are like.

Every good wish from your affectionate . . .

[1] *Madama Butterfly.*

VI

Madama Butterfly

A S THE new opera of Giacomo Puccini *had the honour
of a sole performance* in the largest theatre of
Milan," wrote Giulio Ricordi in the March (1904) number of *Musica e Musicisti*, "few people had the opportunity of seeing and admiring the new scenery, painted
with their accustomed mastery by the Scala scene-painters
after the sketches of Jusseaume, of Paris." And he concluded:

> All the excellent qualities of the *mise en scène* entirely
> escaped the notice of the public, whose preoccupation, indeed,
> was with far other things, with Butterfly's maid, for instance,
> when she goes to pull up the blinds of the large window in
> the background—and this is such an extraordinary thing to do
> that it justified the merriment which it called forth in the
> audience.

Then, in the calendar, "Round the World in a Month,"
of the same review, under the date of February 17, there
appeared the following simple and disdainful account
of the tragic night:

> First performance of *Madama Butterfly*, libretto by Illica
> and Giacosa, music by Puccini. Growls, shouts, groans, laugh-
> ter, giggling, the usual single cries of *bis*, designed specially to
> excite the audience still more: these sum up the reception
> given by the public of the Scala to Giacomo Puccini's new
> work. After this pandemonium, throughout which practically

nothing could be heard, the public left the theatre as pleased as Punch. And one had never before seen so many happy, or such joyously satisfied, faces—satisfied as if by a triumph in which all had shared. In the atrium of the theatre the joy was at its height, and there were those who rubbed their hands, underlining the gesture with the solemn words, *Consummatum est, parce sepulto!* The performance given in the pit seems to have been as well organised as that on the stage, since it too began punctually with the beginning of the opera. This is a true account of the evening, after which the authors, Puccini, Giacosa, and Illica, with the approval of the publishing house, withdrew *Madama Butterfly* and returned the fee for rights of performance to the management of the theatre, notwithstanding the earnest requests of the latter for permission to produce the opera again.

About the disastrous failure of *Butterfly*, which was performed for the first time in two acts, too much has been said and written. A few months after, as is well known, the opera, divided into three acts[1] and with a few slight alterations, had its glorious vindication at Brescia. This performance was due particularly to Tito Ricordi, who, in spite even of his father Giulio's unbelief, had dedicated all his faith and determination to the revival of this work, about which he was enthusiastic.

Madama Butterfly had been adapted as a play by David Belasco from a Japanese story by John Luther Long. Puccini had seen the play acted in English and had been very much struck by it. Immediately on his return from London he spoke of it to Giulio Ricordi and to his

---

[1] The new—and final—arrangement was the division of the second act into two parts, with the curtain after the *intermezzo*.—TRANSLATOR.

librettists, Giacosa and Illica, who at once set to work on the subject. This was not a particularly happy period of Puccini's life. Fate seemed to have set her face against him, for not only was he oppressed by family misfortunes, but he was the victim just then of a motoring accident which nearly cost him his life. On the night of February 25, 1903, when he was returning by motor from Lucca with his wife, Elvira, and Antonio, his son, his car was overturned at a bend in the road. His wife and son, although thrown from the car, were uninjured, but Puccini suffered a fracture of the right tibia, which it took eight long months to cure.

But, while the creation of *Butterfly* had been accomplished in a period of anxiety and physical pain, Puccini had suffered no torture of doubt as to the success of his opera. Never, indeed, were rehearsals carried through with more burning enthusiasm. Poets, publishers, friends, and interpreters were convinced of the coming triumph. The delicate music, the moving drama, could not fail. The short letter (No. 83) written to Rosina Storchio, the unsurpassable and unsurpassed protagonist of the first performance at the Scala, on the very day of the performance, is the clearest proof of this confidence. But, instead, it was a howling fiasco, which left for ever, even after many, many years, a deep bitterness in the composer's spirit.

But his own faith in it was not shaken, if ten days after the famous first night he could write thus to his friend Don Panichelli:

Dear Priest,

You will be horrified by the vile words of the envious Press. Never fear! *Butterfly* is alive and real, and will soon rise again. I say it and believe it with an unalterable faith —you will see—and it will be within a couple of months; I cannot as yet tell you where.

In a few days I am going to Torre, and *may this comfort me for my temporary reverse.* Be of good cheer, as is also your affectionate

G. PUCCINI

On the 28th of May following, in fact, *Butterfly* had her Triumph at the Teatro Grande of Brescia, the artists being Salomea Kruceniski, Zenatello, De Luca, and the conductor Campanini. One month later the triumph was repeated at Buenos Aires, with Toscanini conducting and Rosina Storchio as Butterfly.

69

To Giulio Ricordi

> *Torre del Lago*
> *November 20, 1900*

My dear Signor Giulio,

Among the thousand suggestions which have rained upon me I have found nothing which suits me. Targioni offers me the *Tessitori*,[1] others suggest *Les Misérables*, others the inevitable *Cyrano*, . . . and so on even to the *Lea* of Cavallotti.

I have read *Adolphe* and found it very poor material

[1] *Weavers.*

[140]

indeed—no salient situations except for the scene, proposed by Illica, of the Polish dance with appropriate lament and love-scene; all the rest is a faithful and sincere description of the internal struggles of a man who loves, but is tired of loving, a woman who is older than himself, and whom he does not respect.[1] It is impossible to alter the ending—*i.e.*, find another situation for the end. Either in bed like Mimi or in an armchair like Violetta.

I know that Illica can find a means of introducing some movement and more incident, but the subject is too near to that of *Traviata*, without the youth that shines about the head of Violetta.

The protagonist is already the mother of two boys of about eight or ten years old.

In fact, I have not yet found *my* subject.

I despair of it and am tormented in spirit. If at least some reply would come from New York![2]

The more I think of *Butterfly* the more irresistibly am I attracted. Oh, if only I had it here that I might set to work on it! I think that instead of one act I could make two quite long ones: the first in North America and the second in Japan. Illica could certainly find in the novel everything that is wanted.

I do not understand how Mr Maxwell[3] has *still* not answered.

Just think! I wrote yesterday to d'Annunzio to ask

---

[1] The reference is to *Adolphe*, a novel by Benjamin Constant (1815).—TRANSLATOR.

[2] *I.e.*, to the requests for Belasco's consent to the adaptation of *Madama Butterfly* as a libretto.

[3] Ricordi's representative in New York.

about that *Cecco d'Ascoli* (*The Alchemist*) of which he has spoken so much to me and of which he promised me a scenario! . . . I am coming to Milan soon, towards the end of the month, or at least not later than the beginning of December.

Tonight is the second performance[1] at Bologna. On the first night Giacchetti had no sooner opened her mouth than she lost her voice. I did not wish to appear, but the absurd management refused to listen to me.

The rehearsal of necessary scenes which I had on the day of the performance from eleven o'clock till three (!) was no doubt the cause of her sudden collapse—but the said rehearsal was all too necessary, as neither she nor Caruso had yet taken them seriously.

Caruso was *divine*, Giraldoni better than ever. The staging was *horrible*, the *ensemble* ragged and disconnected, perhaps for lack of rehearsal.

Write and give me, please, some news of yourself.

70

To Giulio Ricordi

> *Cutigliano*
> *August 14, 1901*

Dear Signor Giulio,

Nothing from Giacosa! and the ten days of grace have expired. I cannot go on like this.

Don't you know anything about it?

[1] Of *Tosca*.

We shall leave these heights about the 20th, or the 25th at the latest. Elvira, who seemed to be getting on rather well, has her cough continually now. Let us hope that it is just a cold she has taken! I assure you that my life is far from pleasant! Without work, and with my anxiety about Elvira, I pass days that are anything but joyful!

When I have work to do I hope that at least the weight on my spirit will be lightened a little.

Many, many affectionate greetings from . . .

71

To Giulio Ricordi

Torre del Lago
August 23, 1901

Dear Signor Giulio,
    I am waiting for work, and day by day, hour by hour, I look for the packet from Giacosa, which is taking far too long to come. I shall write him a letter now to stir him up.

Illica writes me that he has some new ideas which he thinks are good. All very well, but meantime I have no work! I positively don't know what to do, and time is flying. Where is Tito? I should like to write to him.

How are you? Did the treatment have the desired effect? Elvira is wonderfully well at the moment.

Can I hope for a visit from you, as you suggested?

Have you no more news of *La Bohème* at Vienna, or of *Tosca* in Paris and Dresden? What a lot of questions!

My regards to all, and, in the hope of meeting you soon in Milan for the *reading*, I send you my most affectionate greetings.

72

To Giulio Ricordi

Torre del Lago
April 23, 1902

My dear Signor Giulio,

And so, hosanna! We must shout it open-throated (if it is true)! I await the arrival of the fruit of this great travail, part of a toilsome structure whose completion is still remote. For my part, I am laying stone on stone and doing my best to make Mr F. B. Pinkerton sing like an American.

I have made a pretty fair recovery. My throat still gives me some trouble. It is a kind of weakness left me by the fever; but I feel myself improving hourly. Illica writes me to interview the Japanese Sada Jacco. If you think it worth while I could take a run over to Milan when she comes. But an interpreter will be necessary; she is sure to speak some European language. . . .

Please put me down for two shares in the Scala.

Kindest regards.

Affectionately yours . . .

[144]

73

To Giulio Ricordi

Torre del Lago
May 3, 1902

My *dear Signor Giulio,*
About *Butterfly* you are right a thousand times; the flower scene must be more *flowery.* However, the duet could begin in stanzas with Suzuki outside and then continue in the way which you suggest, to the greater interest, both scenic and musical, of the piece.

It is a good idea to garland the child with flowers!

I shall write to Giacosa to keep him awake.

I am working (and glad of it) at Act I, and am getting on well. I have composed the passage for the entry of Butterfly, and I am pleased with it.

Apart from the fact that they are slightly Italian in character, both the music and the whole scene of this entry are very effective. I am going slowly, as usual, but working carefully and with deliberation.

Meanwhile, my most affectionate regards.

74

To Giulio Ricordi

Torre del Lago

My dear Signor Giulio,
I have had a visit today from Mme Ohyama, wife of the Japanese Ambassador. She told me a great many interesting things and sang some native songs to me. She has promised to send me some native Japanese music. I sketched the story of the libretto for her, and she liked it, especially as just such a story as Butterfly's is known to her as having happened in real life.

She does not approve of the name *Yamadori*, on the ground that it is feminine and otherwise not appropriate; because in Japan they are accustomed in their plays to use names which suggest, or are suitable to, the various types and characters. The uncle's name of *Yaxonpidé* is wrong too. Similarly the names *Sarundapiko, Izaghi, Sganami*, etc., are all wrong. Mme Ohyama is at Viareggio, where I shall go to see her and take notes of what she sings to me.

She is very intelligent and, although plain, is attractive.
Affectionate regards.

75

To Giulio Ricordi

Torre del Lago

My dear Signor Giulio,
You ask for my news? It is the same as usual.
I am at work on Act II, and—I think—successfully, the
more so as the libretto, with a few small exceptions, is
so well constructed and so logical that I am throwing
myself into it with good will and great pleasure. The
wife of the Japanese Ambassador has called upon me
again several times. She has written to Tokio for some
folk songs, but it will be three months before I can have
them! They will be useful for the other scenes!

When the sun comes back may I hope for a little visit
from you, such as I had a few years ago when I was writing *Bohème?* It would be a good augury for me. My
work is going slowly, but it is good and I have great
hopes of it.

Yours affectionately . . .

76

To Giulio Ricordi

Torre del Lago
September 18, 1902

Dear Signor Giulio,
 Butterfly is going well. I have come through an unpleasantly stormy period. . . . Now it seems that a little calm has returned. So *Butterfly* is going ahead, not *à grande vitesse*, but moving. I am at Act II, but I wish now to begin to orchestrate some of Act I.

 I am receiving urgent letters from Geneva asking for *Tosca*. Please do what you think best. I shall write to them that permission must be obtained from you.

 I was hoping for the Scala! Oh, why is it not possible to give *Manon* there? I should like so much to see that opera well performed. Have you read what a stir *Tosca* made at Montevideo? It was the first time it had been given.

 Kindest regards to yourself and Tito, to Signor Tornaghi, and to Blanc from your affectionate . . .

77

To Giulio Ricordi

Torre del Lago
November 16, 1902

My dear Signor Giulio,
For two days I have been in an absolutely miserable state of mind. Why? Because the libretto, as it stands, is not good from the end of Act II onwards, and the realisation of this has been very painful. Now, however, I am convinced that the opera must be in two acts! ! Don't be frightened!

The Consulate was a great mistake. The action must move forward to the close without interruption, rapid, effective, terrible! In arranging the opera in three acts I was making for certain disaster. You will see, dear Signor Giulio, that I am right.

I have written to Giacosa at Parella saying that either he must come to me or I am going to him.

Do not be worried about the two acts. The first lasts a good hour, the second well over the hour, perhaps an hour and a half. But how much more effective!

With this arrangement I am sure of holding my public and not sending them away disappointed. And we shall have at the same time a new division of opera and a performance that is long enough. I am writing also to Illica.

Send me a line. I am quite decided about this change, and am going ahead with the work.

Yours affectionately . . .

[149]

78

To Giulio Ricordi

Torre del Lago
November 19, 1902

Dear Signor Giulio,

Have no fear! I am sure of my ground! And you will see that you too will be convinced about *Butterfly.* I am sure that the opera, with the division which I have adopted, will be very effective indeed. The dilution of the work with that Consulate act is a mistake. This is a little drama which, once begun, must proceed without interruption to the end. At the moment, however, I am thinking of Giacosa. I have written to him, and he replies that he is at my disposal in Milan. I had wished him to be entirely free for me at Parella, but actually, when I wrote to him, he was starting for Milan. He does not yet know of my decision.

I have written about it to Illica, and this morning he replies that he agrees with me, and makes the same suggestion of cutting out the Consulate act. Only, he would like to keep the three acts—but to drop the curtain and raise it again on the same scene does not seem to me desirable. We shall talk about this again in Milan. I have written to Giacosa inviting him here; I shall see what he replies—but I think that it will be difficult to get him to come. In that case I shall come to Milan.

In the meantime I send you all my affectionate greetings.

[150]

79

To Giulio Ricordi

[*Torre del Lago*]

My dear Signor Giulio,

As Illica writes me about *Butterfly* that he has ideas for the combined act as I wish it to be, he ought to come here—and in a short time, with the help of Giacosa's material, we could do the whole thing. I want to ask you to get a letter sent him, or to write him yourself, telling him to come here at once to me.

If you only knew how I am racking my brains! The work to be done is not great, but it is essential to bind the whole story together with a closer logic than there is in Belasco's play. I am now well into the work, and when I come to Milan (which will be soon) I hope to satisfy you.

Will you please, therefore, tell Illica to come to me here, where it is quiet, and in two or three days the work will be completed.

Kind regards.

80

To Giulio Ricordi

My dear Signor Giulio,

Illica leaves today (Sunday).

The work is finished, and we are satisfied, and more than satisfied, with it. It has turned out splendidly, the action moving forward straight and logically in the most satisfying way. Ah! That act at the Consulate was ruining everything! I am at present orchestrating Act I. I am coming to Milan soon, and I hope that you too will be convinced that the work in its present state is more effective. I am sending you two more photographs.

Kindest greetings.

81

To Giulio Ricordi

Boscolungo
August 29, 1903

Dear Signor Giulio,

I am fat and flourishing again. As far as my leg is concerned, I am getting on not so badly but walking with great difficulty and still with two sticks. My general health is very good. There are two professors here, Ciamician, a distinguished chemist, and Napini, the principal of the University of Bologna, also a chemist, who have subjected my urine to infallible tests and have found *no trace* of glucose, with the result that I am eating the hotel food, including the sweets.

I got Codevilla, of San Michele, to come and look at me. He took off my bandages and unfortunately found a little mobility still in the bones. He said that it is always a lengthy matter, but that cure is certain, although it will be a year and a half at least before I can walk like any other Christian. In spite of that, I told him that I should like to go to Paris; he said that I could go, and that while there I should get a good doctor to give me massage and electric treatment, etc., etc., night and morning, and this I could and will do.

Meanwhile, Mademoiselle the Japanese is waiting, but I could orchestrate Act II in Paris in my spare time. I have very little composition still to do.

I have finished the famous *intermezzo*, which I think is good. From that to the end there is not much to do, and I think that we can fix the production for Lent.

Write.

Kindest regards.

82

To Giulio Ricordi

Paris
Thursday, October 22, 1903

Dear Signor Giulio,

In a few days I shall be back—and I can hardly wait: I am so sick of Paris, especially in this bad weather. My leg is improving fairly well, but I still cannot dispense with the two sticks. The bone is solid but the muscles refuse to support me. How despondent I feel! And for so many reasons!

I am longing to be back in Torre again (and I am going straight there) that I may set to work seriously. I can do absolutely nothing here.

Tosca is filling the theatre, but the critics have arrayed me for sacrifice. Not all of them, however. Even Sardou has been very badly abused, especially by Lalo, of the *Temps*. But he is going to reply to his snarls one of these days in the *Figaro*, and I shall add a word or two. In fact, Sardou's son-in-law came to interview me yesterday about this.

It is my week at the Opéra-Comique: Tuesday, Thursday, and Saturday, *Tosca*, and Friday, *Bohème*.

I have decided, then, to return to Torre for about a month and a half. I can work better there, and shall not be forced to remain indoors all day, as I should have to do if I were at home in Milan, where the stairs are so tiring. In a hotel I should not be able to work, and I have much to do and must do it soon. I shall therefore stay for two days at the Continental and then leave for Torre. I hope to be able to leave here on Tuesday evening and arrive in Milan on Wednesday at three.

Kindest regards.

83

To Rosina Storchio

Milan
February 17, 1904

Dear Rosina,[1]

My good wishes are superfluous!

So true, so delicate, so moving is your great art that the public must succumb to it!

[1] On the day of the disastrous first performance at the Scala.

And I hope that through you I am speeding to victory!
Tonight then—with sure confidence and much affection, dear child!

84

To Rosina Storchio

> *Milan*
> *February 22, 1904*

My dear Rosina,

Here is the photograph which I was to give
you. Forgive me for not sending it at once. I had none
left.

And so, my Butterfly, the love-sick little maiden, would
leave me. You seem in your departure to be taking away
the best, the most poetical part, of my work. I think that
Butterfly without Rosina Storchio becomes a thing without a soul. What a shame! After so many anxious fears,
after pouring out such riches of your keen and delicate
intelligence, to receive the reward of brutality! What a
disgrace it was! But I am sure that this horrible impression will soon be wiped out of our minds, and so, with
warm affection and confidence in the future, I wish you
good luck.

> Ever yours . . .

85

To his Brother-in-law Enrico

Milan
February 24, 1904

Dear Enrico,[1]

Thank you very much for your letter. I hope that Tonino[2] had a good journey and that he has completely recovered from his sickness. I am very well—except for a slightly bitter taste in my mouth! But I hope that that will pass into many other mouths and in a more poisonous form. And this, I think, will not be very far off.

My love to everybody.

86

To Rosina Storchio

Torre del Lago
May 4, 1904

Dear Rosina,

I leave here today for Brescia! May God give me good fortune! I think of you so much! I am always seeing you in your charming presentment of *Butterfly* and hearing again the sweet little voice which has such a sure way to the heart. Perhaps at this very moment you are

[1] Husband of Puccini's sister Dide.—TRANSLATOR.
[2] Puccini's only son, Antonio.—TRANSLATOR.

rehearsing over there.[1] How I should like to be there with you! And how are things going for us? Write me a line to Milan and give me all your news.

Affectionate greetings and all that you can desire for yourself, from

Yours sincerely . . .

87

To Giulio Ricordi

Brescia
Saturday [May, 1904]

Dear Signor Giulio,
　　　　　Rehearsals still going well. The tenor's new passage[2] is good and fills in a gap which needed filling. We've made a cut: the dawn, the *allegro*—i.e., from the *adagio* after the voices from within we are passing to the *già l'alba* of Suzuki.

Kruceniski sings very well, and is not deficient in grace and feeling for the part. She is less expressive certainly than little Storchio. Zenatello's voice seems to me to be more flexible than it was, and his performance fresher. The consul is a little sausagey, but as such he serves to complete the meal. Lucucesca is very good. The secondary parts are excellent. Gianoli is very attractive.

So that's all the news. I forgot to tell you that the chorus girls are monsters!

[1] Buenos Aires, where *Butterfly* was being rehearsed.
[2] Pinkerton's *Addio fiorito asil* in the second part of Act II.

Kindest regards. I hope to see you soon. Greetings also from Tito.

Yours affectionately . . .

88

To his Sister Dide

[*Milan*]
June 11, 1904

Dear Dide,

It went exactly as I had wished: a real and unqualified triumph; the success is greater every evening. I go back on Thursday for the performance they are giving in my honour. Afterwards I go to Acqui, then about the 15th of July to Abetone. What quantities of poison have been swallowed and how much purging done!

Elvira is well, and I am pretty fair. Tell Romelde that I shall write to her. I am very busy because I have to get ready for Abetone, make various purchases, and run about quite a lot; and then I am thinking over and discussing the new libretto, of which I cannot yet disclose the title.

Good-bye. Elvira sends greetings,

Yours . . .

89

To Giulio Ricordi

Torre del Lago
February 23, 1905

My dear Signor Giulio,

I had nothing that could possibly interest you except to tell you that I am busy revising.

I should have liked to send you news of a fresh work —but alas, I see much darkness ahead of me! Shall I ever find a subject? I must! Never have I felt as now the swift flight of time, never as now had such a fierce desire to go on. But *on*, not back!

With a work, that is, modern in construction, and *moving*.

I have Act I of *Edgar* ready. Should I send it? or wait till the work is completed?

I have read the review of Bracco's new comedy. I am asking Tito if he doesn't think it a good subject, but certainly not in four acts—in three. It is an idea. I am keeping well. I am getting letters from Maestro Setti in Cairo, where *Butterfly* has had a great success. Nine calls after Act II.

All good wishes, also to Tito, from yours . . .

90

To Giulio Ricordi

> *Torre del Lago*
> *March 21, 1905*

My dear Signor Giulio,
    I was thinking of wiring for news of you when I had your delightful letter. As regards *Edgar*, do all that you think desirable in the matter of scenery, libretto, and staging.

If I were to do *William Tell* I should again be a mark for the thunderbolts of all the Italian critics. Poor, crushed Butterfly! With what feline rage did they hurl themselves upon her! Well, the need is urgent to find a libretto, whether comic or serious. *But I must have one!* This can't go on any longer! ! And my poets? Alas and alack!

> Ever yours . . .

91

To his Sister Tomaide

> *Via Verdi, 4*
> *Milan*
> *April 24, 1905*

Dear Tomaide,
    Thank you for your good wishes which are also ours to you. In the beginning of June I go to Buenos

Aires and return in August. I am going by invitation, with passage paid for Elvira and me and 50,000 francs in addition! As you will know, they are giving five operas of mine there, and I am going specially to produce *Edgar*, which will be performed by the best artists. Then in autumn at Bologna they are giving *Butterfly*, as also at the Dal Verme in Milan, at Covent Garden in London, and then at Naples. So you see, my star is burning bright— with *Edgar*!

I am well. I hope to see you soon. It is likely that I shall make a flying visit to Tuscany before I leave, and in that case we shall meet at Lucca.

Good-bye. Elvira sends her regards.

Yours . . .

92

To his Sister Nitteti

> *Naples*
> *January 26, 1906*

Dear Nitteti,

I am here for *Butterfly*, which has achieved a really great triumph.

Poor little Carlo! I hope that the improvement will soon begin. I think of you, poor child, and how you must suffer to see him like that! I shall leave here on Tuesday to go straight to Milan, and I do not know if I shall be able to come to Torre this March. I must go to Nice and then to Palermo. This life is very wearing to me! But my presence in the theatres is necessary.

Love to Carlino and Alba.

Yours . . .

93

To his Sister Nitteti

> *Paris*
> *November 14, 1906*

Dear Nitteti,

Elvira is here with me and will write to you. We speak of you so often, and I should like to write to you, but I never find the time.

Do not believe that I am so very well. I have some very bad days. My accursed diabetes gives me a great deal of trouble.

We shall be ready for the performance in the beginning of December. How it bores me to stay here so long! I should like to be at Torre or Chiatri, in solitude and peace.

Butterfly continues her triumphal career: Washington, Baltimore, Boston, and yesterday, New York—always in English. In January I am going to New York for *Manon, Butterfly, Tosca,* and then *Butterfly* in Italian at another theatre, the great Metropolitan.

But first I shall return to Italy if only for a few days. I have to come, besides, for clothes. I must get a fur-lined coat because it is very cold in New York.

And if I come in the direction of Torre I shall visit you and see for myself the improvement in little Carlo. You must not despair. Cheer up and keep a brave heart. In March I shall have some peace. How distant that is! I ought not to have accepted the invitation to America, but now that I have, *il faut y aller.*

Elvira will write to you tomorrow. Good-bye. Love to Carlino and yourself from Elvira and me.

Yours . . .

94

To Giulio Ricordi

Paris
November 15, 1906

Dear Signor Giulio,

       I hasten to reply to your telegram just received. Immediately on the arrival of your first telegram I commissioned the translation of Wilde's *Tragedy.* It will be well done—in French. As regards the collaboration, I am in *no* way bound. On the contrary, after the annoyance suffered over *La Conchita,* I do not feel inclined to put myself again in the same position.

By this time, as I have said, the commission has been given, and I cannot withdraw it.

The people here are in no hurry. Carré's fussiness about the *mise en scène* (his wife has to be considered too) is enough to turn one's hair grey.

[163]

Well, I must be patient. But when shall we be ready? They say at the beginning of December. I hope so.

I wrote to Illica last night frankly and uncompromisingly; we shall see with what result.

I am not feeling too well. I am continually very much depressed and with no reason. . . . The thought, also, of going to America is getting on my nerves. Why ever did I accept?

How glad I'd feel to be back in Torre del Lago with my free life and the fresh air! . . .

If they are going to be so late with this *première* I shall barely have the time (and I shall be lucky if I have it) to return to Italy and pack up again at once.

If only I could at least have a week or two of quietness!

They are preparing the opera very well, and already, in these even partial rehearsals, they are all convinced that it will be a great success.

The music which one hears in Paris just now is frightful. *Aphrodite*[1] is marvellous scenically, but there isn't a page which one can understand. It is absolutely horrible stuff: a little colour and a conglomeration of perfectly hideous sounds. Debussy's *Pelléas et Mélisande* has extraordinary harmonic qualities and the most delicate instrumental effects. It is very interesting, in spite of its colouring, which is sombre and unrelieved like a Franciscan's habit.

The subject is interesting. None of the other new

[1] Opera by Camille Erlanger, produced in 1906.—TRANSLATOR.

operas that are being given are worth talking about. Hence it will be difficult to succeed with *Butterfly*.

Every affectionate greeting from

Yours . . .

95

To Giulio Ricordi

Paris
Sunday evening

Dear Signor Giulio,

Tomorrow is the first rehearsal *à l'italienne*— *i.e.*, with everybody, including the orchestra, but no scenery. Immediately after that we begin the full rehearsals, including the acting.

I have the score here, almost ready, and tomorrow it will be finished. With regard to the *mise en scène*, am I to leave it as it is, or have the most important things changed? Carré has altered nearly everything, and with good results. There is even a new cut in Act II: that bit about the *bravo giudice*[1] before tea. Shall I mark the cut and make it final? With the new *mise en scène*, that passage seems to me entirely superfluous. Everything has been well rehearsed, and I hope that the performance will be very good indeed. The third act, as Carré does it, taking away most of her part from Kate and leaving her outside in the garden—which is on the stage level and has still no hedge, and so no awkward barrier—pleases

---

[1] The authorised English version has "the true, honest, and unbiased judge."

me very much. The final scene too is excellent. We shall have wonderful effects of light and flowers. The whole of the first act is put on with fine judgment. The arrival of the Bonze is very effective. Appearing from a height, and hurling himself upon the scene across the bridge (by which Butterfly too arrives), he utters his curse with enormous effect, for one after another, the mother, cousin, aunts, and friends, while the Bonze is vomiting his diatribes, throw themselves in his path with suppliant gestures, but are violently *repoussées* by the fierce uncle until he reaches Butterfly. Then the tenor intervenes with a protest. The marriage takes place in the little house, where Butterfly remains kneeling, while the Japanese Commissioner kneels also in front of a little lacquer writing-desk. While they drink a toast to Kami-Kami, Goro lights some fireworks.

The flower scene is danced almost throughout. Yamadori does not enter the room, but sits down considerately to wait, on the step leading up from the garden; for I must explain that the floor of the room is raised about a foot and a half above the stage level and that on this platform they have put a little row of footlights and have covered the front elevation with flowers. And so the garden is about a foot and a half lower.

Yesterday I was at the Italian Embassy, where they gave a great dinner. Clemenceau was there; so were old Di Rudinì, Carré, and many others. In the course of a conversation Carré told me that he was certain that the opera would make a great impression.

[166]

There is much talk of Carré as director of the Grand Opéra.

I have written to Illica about the *Florentine Tragedy*, and he has replied that he is keen to do it. I have the copy, and we shall have no collaborator at all.

Vaucaire had already written to me about it, but I cut the matter short by saying that I did not wish to be involved again in the fuss and difficulties experienced over *Conchita*.[1] Talking of *Conchita*, I have invited Louys and Vaucaire to dinner, in the hope of deciding, if possible about that curtain.

Floquet[2] says that up to now he has concluded for this winter sixteen agreements for *Tosca*, and that this is the most successful year we have had in France. Carré would willingly take *Tosca* again, but he has no tenor, and he has asked me if I know a good Italian artist who sings in French. Do you know any?

I have had newspapers from New York. All very favourable.

At the moment I have nothing more to tell you. I shall write after further rehearsals. The *première* will be in the first week of December.

Affectionate greetings.

[1] *Conchita* was an opera, projected but not completed, based on Pierre Louys' novel *La Femme et le pantin*.—TRANSLATOR.

[2] Floquet was then representing the house of Ricordi in Paris.

96

To Tito Ricordi

New York
February 18 [1907]

Dear Tito,

Butterfly went very well as far as the Press
and public were concerned, *but not so as to please me.* It
was a performance without poetry. Farrar is not too satisfactory. She sings out of tune, forces her voice, and it
does not *carry* well in the large space of the theatre. I
had to struggle to obtain two full-dress rehearsals, including the general![1] Nobody knew anything. Dufrich
had not taken the trouble to study the *mise en scène*,
because the composer was there. Vigna did his best but
he can't control his orchestra. As long as he had me at
his elbow things went very well, but whenever I left the
field there were disasters.

However, it went well, on the whole, and the Press is
unanimous in its praise. This is the first day that I have
been able to write after six days of influenza which *m'a
tué.* I am sailing on the 26th in the *Kronprinz.* I wanted
to go to Niagara, but now I have neither the desire nor
the time to go.

Now there is the question of *Conchita.* I am still terribly doubtful about this subject. When I think of the
novel I have no doubt, but when I think of the libretto

---

[1] This is the rehearsal to which in France, Italy, and America critics and
others are invited.—TRANSLATOR.

[168]

I have many. Its structure and its dangerous and far from clear psychology frighten me.

Conchita never succeeds in standing out with the clear picture which she makes in Pierre Louys' story.

The development lacks colour, and is frightfully difficult and dangerous to represent musically, with the variety which is necessary in the theatre. The first and second scenes are all right, but the scene at the window in the dance-*café* and the last scene are both, in my opinion, unsatisfactory. Let us ponder it well, because I shall never be able to set to work on a subject, if I am not fully convinced about it first—for my own sake and for yours. Are you, with your discernment in matters theatrical, convinced of it?

Examine this *boat* all over, and see if you find any leaks. I can see them. And what am I to do? The world is expecting an opera from me, and it is high time it were ready. We've had enough now of *Bohème, Butterfly*, and Co.! Even I am sick of them! But I really am greatly worried! I am tormented not for myself alone, but for you, for Signor Giulio, and for the house of Ricordi to whom I wish to give and must give an opera that is sure to be good.

Here too I have been on the lookout for subjects, but there is nothing possible, or rather, complete enough. I have found good ideas in Belasco, but nothing definite, solid, or complete.

The "West" attracts me as a background, but in all the plays which I have seen I have found only some scenes here and there that are good. There is never a clear, simple line of development; just a hotch-potch and sometimes in very bad taste and very *vieux jeu*.

I have written all this by way of preparing you, that you may not suffer an unpleasant surprise when I expose my doubts about *Conchita*.

You will say, of course, "Why ever did you fasten on to the subject then?" My dear fellow, I have been torturing my brains and my spirit for three years to find a place to lay my four notes, and have fastened with feline hunger on the subject which has impressed me more than any other. The book is beautiful—but the libretto, or rather, the theatrical lay-out, is imperfect, because I realise that it is *impossible* to reproduce for the stage the speech and action of the original.

The scene of the naked dance must be disguised. The virginity question, which is the crux of the book, *cannot* be made clear in a *spoken* version of the story.

I am afraid of the last scene, which, if it is not exceptionally realistic, is only an ordinary duet. And this scene is perilous and, in the form in which I have imagined it, will not be accepted by the public. In short, I assure you that my life is not all roses, and this state of mental excitement is making my existence nervous and my humour most melancholy.

Before I leave, I am to have an interview with Belasco, but I do not expect much from it. Song, too, whom I met in Philadelphia the other night at the second performance of *Butterfly*, wishes to suggest a subject to me. I am going to see a powerful drama of Belasco's called *The Music Master*, and another by Hauptmann of which I have heard good reports. Then I have finished and I shall see you soon again in Milan.

I do need a rest! After Paris, New York—I've had enough of it!

Kindest regards to you and your father.

VII

La Fanciulla del West

LIKE *Butterfly*, *La Fanciulla del West* was derived from a play by David Belasco.

While staying in Paris on his way to New York[1] Puccini met his friend Piero Antinori, who was himself returning from New York. It was he who urged Puccini to go to see the new play which had been running for some months with enormous success at the Belasco Theatre, and which was called *The Girl of the Golden West*. Puccini was greatly impressed by the play: the very dramatic story, the strong, exotic colouring, the primitive blend of brutality and sweetness, and the well-designed grouping of the figures attracted him at once. The negotiations with Belasco, by this time a great admirer and devoted friend of Puccini's, were quickly completed. On his return to Italy, Puccini, with the publisher's consent, arranged with Carlo Zangarini for the composition of the libretto.[2] Naturally, Belasco's play had to undergo considerable transformation, especially in Act III, which was planned entirely according to the ideas and desires of the composer. The work was neither easy nor short. To the name of Zangarini was added that of Guelfo Civinini, a man of swift and sure theatrical

[1] Probably in 1906.—TRANSLATOR.
[2] The death of Giuseppe Giacosa in 1906 dissolved the famous partnership of Puccini, Giacosa, and Illica.—TRANSLATOR.

instinct and a very exquisite poet. And thus was born
La Fanciulla del West, strong and beautiful and
irresistible.

Puccini had promised the first right of production of
the opera to Gatti Casazza, for the New York Metropolitan, where Arturo Toscanini was then acting as artistic director; and the Metropolitan prepared to give the
composer a very festive welcome.

Puccini left for America in time for the first rehearsals
in November, 1910, on the *George Washington*. He was
accompanied by his son Antonio and the publisher Tito
Ricordi. It was a happy voyage, full of hopes which were
not disappointed. The rehearsals were carried out in an
atmosphere of the utmost friendliness. Toscanini, Tito
Ricordi, and Belasco himself were there, as well as Gatti
Casazza, who worked in enthusiastic collaboration with
Puccini. The *mise en scène* was wonderful and the execution beyond praise. The cast included Caruso, Destinn,
Amato, Didur, and Pini-Corsi.

After two general rehearsals, which had aroused great
enthusiasm, the first performance, on the evening of
December 10, 1910, proved to be one of the Metropolitan's biggest events. The takings had reached an
astounding figure, and the triumph of Giacomo Puccini
was unqualified and complete. The success was such that
the prices for the second performance were doubled.

The first performance in Italy was given on the evening of June 12, 1911, at the Costanzi in Rome. Both
public and critics were enthusiastic. Giovanni Pozza,
writing in the *Corriere della Sera*, declared that Puccini

had "never shown such a sure control of his genius and his skill as in this opera." And, speaking of the harmonic graces of the work, he said that the score was "sprinkled with them as a meadow with flowers," and that Puccini's was "the palette of a great painter." All agreed that Puccini had once more "vindicated his right to be included among the greatest Italian composers of opera, his power of rhythm and his mastery of the unity of combined masses of sound being not only elements, but often protagonists in the drama."

In the *Secolo* Gaetano Cesari praised the variety and skill of the instrumentation, in which was evident the sure and happy choice of the combinations best calculated to achieve the colour which he desired.

At the production in the Costanzi the soprano was Burzio, Bassi was the tenor, and Amato the baritone. Toscanini conducted.

97

To Giulio Ricordi

Torre del Lago
July 15, 1907

Dear Signor Giulio,
  I had already written to Maxwell instructing him to ask Belasco for his terms, and to add that it would be necessary to omit a great part of the play and to do a considerable amount of creative work in the reconstruction; and that if his terms were impossible I should go

no further, etc., etc. If you would write to Maxwell too, it would help. I send you Acts III and IV. They are not of much use to us, however. They must be entirely rearranged and rewritten. If we do that it will be possible to get something good out of them. We must somehow or other keep the *class di asen*,[1] to which I should tack on the fourth act, with the lovers walking away over the open country, and scenery half interior and half out of doors; the exterior of the house to have a large veranda. But it is winter! And people do not live in the open in winter! What shall we do about that? When you have read the play I would suggest passing it on to Zangarini.

Read it then, please, and tell me at once what you think.

Yours affectionately . . .

98

To Giulio Ricordi

Torre del Lago
September 14, 1907

Dear Signor Giulio,

Zangarini is in constant touch with me, and in a few days is coming to me with material. I have not gone to sleep, nor am I letting myself grow cold on the subject of the *West*—far from it! I am thinking of it constantly and I am certain that it will prove to be a

[1] The "Donkeys' Class," the scene in which Minnie gives a lesson to the miners. The expression is Milanese, and is the title of a comedy in dialect by Ferravilla.—TRANSLATOR.

second *Bohème*, unless my brain and energy fail me. I am not abandoning the idea of Marie Antoinette. Have you read Illica's first act? Tell me what I am to do about it. It will be necessary to criticise it rather severely for its extreme laconicism, as well as for its form. He must have a collaborator. How am I to tell him? I await your advice.

Yours affectionately . . .

99

To Giulio Ricordi

Boscolungo
Sunday

    My dear Signor Giulio,

       We are getting on! The *Girl* promises to become a second *Bohème*, but more vigorous, more daring, and on an altogether larger scale. I have in mind a magnificent scenario, a clearing in the great Californian forest, with some colossal trees. But we shall need eight or ten horses on the stage.

    Zangarini is now in the incubation period. Let's hope that the result will be good.

    I am going down to Lucca in a few days for some rehearsals of *Butterfly*.

Yours . . .

100

To Giulio Ricordi

[Naples]
February 2, 1908

Dear Signor Giulio,
　　I hope that you have recovered from your illness of a few days ago. I sail at nine o'clock tonight. The steamer is magnificent.

Last night I was able to go to the *première* of *Salome*, conducted by Strauss, and sung (?) by Bellincioni, whose dancing is marvellous. It was a success. . . . But there must be many who doubt the verdict. The playing of the orchestra was like a badly mixed Russian salad. But the composer was there, and everybody says that it was perfect.

I am reading the *Fanciulla* and coming to the conclusion that Zangarini has done it *well*. Of course there are some points, both literary and scenic, which will have to be corrected, and I shall write my criticisms in the margin. I am already savouring in advance the moment when I shall finally set to work! Never have I had such a fever for it as now!

I shall write to you from Cairo, and will take as many photographs as I can. I am travelling with two cameras like any Montabone![1]

The weather here is wretched. Let's hope that the sea

---

[1] A well-known photographer.—TRANSLATOR.

won't be too rough. Not for me, but for Elvira, who is always so ill.

Clausetti is very well and sends kind regards. They are now going to give a shortened *Tosca* and afterwards *Bohème*, also shortened.

At the rehearsals, when Strauss was trying to work up his orchestra to a rough and tempestuous kind of execution, he said, "Gentlemen, this is not a question of music, but of a menagerie. Make a noise! Blow into your instruments!" What do you think of that?

Kindest greetings to you and Tito and everybody from
Yours affectionately . . .

101

To Guelfo Civinini

*Milan
April 11, 1908*

My dear Civinini,
You will have heard from Tito Ricordi that the collaboration[1] has been arranged.

I am leaving today for Torre del Lago. I await anxiously our first meeting. Will you come to Torre?

Meantime, as I have the copy, you can begin to study it with a view to an economical reduction of Act I, which I think is too long, especially in the card scene, and try to make it clearer and more living and convincing. How

---

[1] This letter followed immediately on the completion of the agreement with Ricordi for the collaboration of Guelfo Civinini with Zangarini.

pleased I should be if you were to bring with you to Torre your ideas already written down and some changes already made!

I am in the most anxious haste to set to work.

Sincerely yours . . .

102

To Guelfo Civinini

Torre del Lago
April 29, 1908

My dear Civinini,

When are those chattering women going to finish?[1] I am in a hurry to see you. I beg you to come here immediately. Time is flying, and the oil is burning out!

Sincerely yours . . .

103

To Guelfo Civinini

Milan
May 31, 1908

Dear Guelfo,

I am awaiting the revised proofs of Act I. Did you get the manuscript which refers to the text?

[1] A famous congress of women was meeting at this time in Rome. Civinini was attending on behalf of the *Corriere della Sera*, and so could not go to Puccini.

I am still here because I am ill, not seriously, but I have to be inconveniently careful of myself and stay in bed, which prevents me from working or moving about. We could shorten Act I in some other places besides the duet. Will you look and see? Don't you think when Nick has once said that the boys guard the treasure by night that he could stop saying it? And in the duet I should mention the redemption only once.

Write and give me news of Act III.

Yours affectionately . . .

104

To Giulio Ricordi

Chiatri
July 13, 1908

My dear Signor Giulio,

Your very welcome letter has been forwarded to me up here. *I am well*—I am working. Civinini has replied at last. He says that he has begun Act III but that he needs a week near me and will come to Abetone.[1] I am shaping my material as best I can and trying to get ahead. It is a very difficult piece of work, this *Girl* (I shall never call it *Fanciulla*, if only because of the two last syllables, which I am afraid might refer to me[2]). I am sorry that the Signora Giuditta has been ill again.

[1] Puccini was going to Boscolungo in the Abetone for the summer.—TRANSLATOR.

[2] The word *ciullo* is sometimes used to mean "stupid."—TRANSLATOR.

I hope that she is keeping better now. Please give my kindest regards to her and to Signorina Ginetta, to whom I send also my best wishes for a complete recovery. And Tito? Is he lost?

Yours affectionately . . .

105

To Guelfo Civinini

Boscolungo Pistoiese
August 10, 1908

Dear Civico,
I have received the manuscript, sent on here. Thank you for having worked. Much of it I think good, but there are other parts which I think will have to be changed. There are too many solo parts for men of the chorus. I should have liked groups of seven or eight men rushing in and making a noise, etc., but we must discuss this when we meet. There are rooms here with board for twelve lire a day. I cannot ask you to come to me, because my little house is full—there is even some one sleeping on a sofa! But I assure you that in a few days I shall leave here, because I am not comfortable, and I am not working. I want to go down to Chiatri or Torre or Viareggio. Tell me if you could not postpone your holiday till October or the end of September, and come to Torre, where we can do our work between a shoot on the lake and a run out to sea in a motor-boat. If, however, you

want the hill air, I shall stay here and not go away just yet.

Write soon.

Yours affectionately . . .

106

To Guelfo Civinini

Boscolungo Pistoiese

Dear Civinini,

Did I tell you? It is raining continually here, and we are leaving for Torre del Lago on Wednesday. You should therefore come soon, and we shall fix up Act III, to my joy and yours, not to speak of our dear Uncle Giulio, who writes me that he is wasting away like a burning candle.

Yours sincerely . . .

107

To Guelfo Civinini

Boscolungo Pistoiese
August 18, 1908, Evening

Dear Civinini,

I have today had the notice of the dispatch of a packet which it will be a great joy to receive; you know my weakness. I am leaving on Thursday, the day after tomorrow, for Torre del Lago, and I am thankful to depart from a place where I have been bored and felt ill, have not worked, have been cold, etc., etc.

I guess from your letter that you are coming *soon* to Torre. Come and we shall enjoy ourselves. You shall work, and we'll go shooting. Come, come.

Kindest greetings and many thanks from
Yours sincerely . . .

108

To Guelfo Civinini

Torre del Lago
September 21, 1908

Dear Civ.,

Elvira and I thank you so much for what you have written to us. I am working now, but I am not in a mood for it. I am not feeling well, and, in fact, am going to see Gracco to be examined either tomorrow or next day.

Look at the rhymes in the first two lines of Act III, *Rance* and *mance*.[1] You must correct that. Here life is as usual; shooting—*nada*; I shall take photographs for *La Lettura*.[2] In those of Pascoli there was a blank film. I am destined not to succeed in taking a photograph of the

---

[1] In the opera the name Rance retained the American pronunciation, and therefore could not rhyme with the Italian *mance*.—TRANSLATOR.

[2] A literary review published by the *Corriere* of Milan.—TRANSLATOR.

poet. Remember the label to cover up the word *Abetone* on your letters.

Many affectionate greetings from
Yours . . .

109

To Giulio Ricordi

Chiatri (Lucca)

Dear Signor Giulio,

You are right! Oh, those librettists! One has disappeared, and the other does not even answer my letters. And I am here trying to make shift as best I can. But I can do little by myself. This first act is long and full of details of no particular interest! . . . I really need *one* of them here with me to follow my directions conscientiously. How am I to manage? I am discouraged, because I should like to make cuts, but they must be made systematically and with proper connections; and this I cannot do unaided.

Affectionate greetings.

110

To Giulio Ricordi

Torre del Lago
July 28, 1910

Dear Signor Giulio,
The opera is finished!
I have done a little cutting and left out some rather nice but useless things from the libretto. This was done *at midnight.* I assure you, that as it now stands, it is emotionally, as well as scenically and in its fine conclusion, a work that will matter. It was last night, with me as judge and Carignani as counsel, that the case of Minnie and her friends was concluded.
God be praised!
Yours affectionately . . .

111

To Giulio Ricordi

November 10, 1910

My dear Signor Giulio,
Here we are, actually at sea.[1] We have what is called the Imperial Suite.
A princely bath, a room with two gilt bedsteads with various sorts of opaline-tinted lamps; drawing-room with

[1] He was setting out for New York to attend the rehearsals and production of the opera.

luxurious divans and mikado mirrors; dining-room with furniture in the best English taste, ingenious cupboards which are even lighted inside, everything comfortable, large, and spacious as in the most modern of hotels. Price, £320 for passage alone. Large windows with sumptuous silk curtains. In short, a stupendous suite! Praise be to the Metropolitan!

Up to now the sea exhibits a calm worthy of the Emperor of China.

Tito has good quarters too, but he spends all (or nearly all) his time with us, lounging on our cushions and imperial sofas; we are served by special *garçons* who come running at every nod like so many lackeys.

I believe that even you, who so hate the sea, would enjoy this. The *Washington* has a tonnage of 36,000 and is 715 feet long. Colossal! Monumental! But enough of this for the present. Take care of yourself; I hope to find you on my return completely restored to health, and that the success of the *Girl* will have given you cause for rejoicing.

All best wishes from us to you and Signora Giuditta.

VIII

La Rondine

WHEN Giacomo Puccini, yielding to the persuasions of the two directors of the Karltheater in Vienna, decided to compose an operetta he in all probability had the presentiment already that he never would compose an operetta. It is significant that while, from one point of view, the project amused him, he protected himself, on the other hand, by reserving all the rights of production in Italy and South America. Operetta, yes, if possible—but only for foreign countries.

A few months after—it was in 1914—the first draft of the libretto, submitted by the Viennese publishers, was uncompromisingly rejected. That was already a step backwards. But Berté and Eisenschitz, although they had not yet entered into a definite contract with Puccini, did not give up hope. They instructed Willner and Reichert to find another subject in Puccini's vein, and all four made the journey to Milan to lay before the composer the scenario of *La Rondine*.[1] Puccini did not there and then dislike it. The contract was concluded, and publishers and librettists returned to Vienna satisfied that they had got what they wanted.

Soon after, however, matters suddenly took a different turn.

Puccini had commissioned Giuseppe Adami to write

[1] *The Swallow.*

the libretto according to the canons of operetta—*i.e.*, in prose and verse[1]—and, of course, in Italian. The Viennese librettists were then to make the German translation. Puccini set to work, putting first one fragment, then a second, to music; then, when he was just arriving at the third, one fine day he could do no more, and told Adami definitely there and then that he would never compose an operetta.

It was thus that the plot of *La Rondine*, devised for an operetta, suffered transformation into a libretto for opera.

For the first act things went well. The light and delicate story lent itself to a setting that was full of life and colour. But in the succeeding acts the transformation was a laborious and wearying process. On every side arose insidious and unexpected difficulties not easy to overcome, and increased by the fact that the outbreak of the Great War had not only made communication with the Viennese collaborators impossible, but had rendered still more intolerable this contract with Austrian publishers, who refused to cancel it.

Thus *La Rondine* was born under no happy star, and it was unfortunate also that the transformation in the libretto did not succeed in concealing its somewhat hybrid origin. Puccini had poured into the work a limpid and scintillating stream; he had made a score full of beauty and charm and technically perfect. Yet the opera

---

[1] The operetta, of which *Die Fledermaus* of Johann Strauss is an example, is not necessarily short, but is of a lighter character than opera: it has comic elements and the dialogue is spoken.—TRANSLATOR.

A Curious Letter of the "La Rondine" Period Signed
by Puccini with a Caricature Sketch of His Own Head

It reads: "Dear Adami,—Time is passing—the drums are rolling. I wanted
to finish—you know it. What about it? Yours . . ."

lacked the vitality which the first performance at Monte Carlo, on March 27, 1917, had led one to expect. Then it had had a very real success. The interpretation, entrusted in the principal parts to della Rizza, the tenor Schipa, Ines Maria Ferraris, and Dominici, was excellent. The critics unanimously recognised the musical importance of the opera. In May of the same year, under the direction of Panizza, *La Rondine* had a triumph even in Italy, in the comunale of Bologna. After this several mediocre performances did nothing to help the opera, which languished still more after the far from praiseworthy performance which it had in the Volksoper at Vienna.

Nevertheless, Puccini was always convinced that *La Rondine*, one day or another, would resume her flight—above all, if he could find a theatre suited to the small proportions of the opera and interpreters of sufficient freshness and ability, both of which he had had at Monte Carlo.

The long toil by which this subject was worked out, and to which the letters here collected bear witness, continued even for some years after the first performance. Musically, too, the opera was retouched several times by the composer, who loved to linger over the sparkling music with a kind of tenderness for this child of his which had not succeeded, like the others, in filling the theatres of Italy and the rest of the world.

(All the letters included in this section were written to Giuseppe Adami.)

112

Torre del Lago
Sunday [*1914 (?)*]

My *dear Adami,*

Thank you for your letter with its good news of our work. Do get on with it! For my part, the more I think of it, the more interesting I find it and full of alluring things. Please pay special attention to the third act. It must be great; it must grip and move its hearers. It must be the *climax*, where all the dominant forces of the drama have their expression. We are clear about Act I. Get on with the work now, while the impression is fresh. We shall meet again when your general plan is outlined; either come here or I shall come to you. Nothing yet, from Vienna. Eisner[1] has written to Tito,[2] but saying nothing definite, it seems. About Ouida, it seems that there is no proprietor in London. Tomorrow I am seeing at Viareggio a solicitor who was the executor of the authoress and to whom I have been directed from London.[3]

Affectionate greetings. It is cold and wet here.

Yours . . .

[1] Baron Eisner, of Vienna, acted as intermediary between Puccini and the Austrian publisher.

[2] Tito Ricordi was now directing the publishing house, his father having died in 1912.—TRANSLATOR.

[3] Puccini had in mind an opera based on Ouida's *Two Little Wooden Shoes.* —TRANSLATOR.

113

> *Torre del Lago*
> *April 3, 1914, 2 A.M.*

My dear Adami,

I hope to be in Milan on Thursday. Willner will be there, and the three of us will pull and stretch our stuffs to see if we can improve them.

Meanwhile, refurbish and examine the *Two Little Wooden Shoes*, whose copyright lasts till 1958! This is my latest information. I have written to confirm everything. I am waiting for the *Corriere*, to get the news about Alfano.[1] I hope that it will be good.

> Sincerely yours . . .

114

> *Viareggio*
> *Friday, September 25, 1914*

Dear Adami,

I do not say that Act II is ugly, slovenly, or untheatrical. No, not that. But I do say that it is not . . . very beautiful, that in form it is not very perfect, that it is not . . . super-drama as it should be. As I read the review of Labiche's vaudeville, *Le Chapeau de Paille*, my heart was wrung. Why? Because our work lacks vitality

---

[1] Alfano's new opera, *L'Ombra di Don Giovanni*, which had a moderate success at the Scala.

and the varying intrigue and the changing vicissitudes which are essential if we are to interest and amuse the public. We must amuse the *organ-grinder*, my dear Adami. If not, we fail utterly, and that must not happen. Act I is good, and Act III will be excellent. But Act II won't do at all, *tout cru*! Let's send Bullier to the devil! Let's find another scene, more alive, more varied, more full of colour, if possible. I have nothing to suggest off-hand; but I judge from that feeling which weighs upon my spirit as I work that our labours are not prospering. I am not happy, I am not laughing, I am not interested. We need something better than this, dear Beppino, in our weary world! . . . We need, that is, a second act. And let us make it while there is still time. We shall keep the principal episodes. But we must create some new and interesting ones. Pardon the diatribe, which is not against you, but against myself rather.

Affectionately yours . . .

115

Torre del Lago
October 4, 1914

Dear Adamino,

We are at Torre, but with no servants! They were dismissed at once when we left Viareggio, both the cook and the man. We go for lunch and dinner to Viareggio and sleep at Torre. My melancholy is immense, unspeakable, frightening!

I am working, but very inconclusively, because the second act is not as I want it to be. I do little bits here and there. I cannot tell you to come for the present, since we are in this state of disorder. But as soon as we are straight it will be a great joy to have you here.

Tonio was to come back, but instead he is saying no more about it. I have had no news of him for five days! You can imagine how black my mood is!

Many, many greetings to you and to your wife and little one from your very unhappy and almost *ex* . . .

116

Torre del Lago
Wednesday, October 14, 1914

Dear Adamino,
        I am still without a cook. In a few days (the 19th) I shall have one, and then you shall come and we shall make the necessary alterations in Act II. My spirits are still plunged in their accustomed gloom. When you are here we shall send for the Siamese twins Caramba and Rovescalli.[1]

I have done very little work. I have touched up the libretto here and there. But you will see when you come.
        Affectionately yours . . .

[1] These two artists are constantly associated as designers of costumes and scenery.—TRANSLATOR.

117

> *Torre del Lago*
> *November 10, 1914*

Dear Adamino,

That bore Carignani is here. There is a sun fit to split the pavements. I have left the quartet for the moment, in order to fill up [*colmare*] other gaps, other *lacunae*—for lagoons[*lacune*] are filled with the sea [*col mare*]. But the sea must go into the quartet, and if you don't make me the *stanze*[1] we shall have to sleep out of doors—and you know that the cold is beginning now, in spite of the sun that is splitting. . . . The first woodcocks have made their appearance, and coot-shooting is continuing, to the great annoyance of the neighbourhood. But what is concerning me is that you should not give me *white hairs* by holding up the third act and the stanzas that I am waiting for. And while I am on the subject I may as well tell you of the pleasure and emotion which I felt when I read your *White Hairs*[2] in Venice. I wish you, when its time comes, all the success which you deserve. Can you find a way to write me the few lines which I need for the quartet? Then I think that we can finish the opera.

> Yours . . .

[1] A play on the double sense of the Italian *stanza*: (1) room, (2) stanza.—Translator.

[2] *I Capelli Bianchi*, a comedy in three acts, by Giuseppe Adami.—Translator.

118

Torre del Lago
November 11, 1914

Dear Adami,

I knew already all the arguments which you have written to me. Now here is how the matter stands: We must keep this plot, but we must make it less harsh. So I am going ahead, and as I find that in the second act there is too little animation and none of the gaiety and cheerful noise that there should be, considering where the scene is laid, I have had the idea of lengthening the waltz by adding some music which will be livelier and have more *entrain* in it. This music I have, in fact, composed. It now only wants the *mise en scène*. This lively music must have its counterpart in some scene of unrestrained gaiety. And we need words. At a certain point the two lovers break into the love-song in waltz time, and this, I think, is going to fit in well. We have still to consider the third act. Meanwhile, I am going ahead. There is an Achilles' heel also in the first act: Magda not seen by Ruggero. When I reread the libretto *I did not like this.* I think, however, that, now that everything else is satisfactorily arranged, it will be possible to add a few words for Magda and make her go out, and come back again at the moment when Lisette is showing Ruggero out.

Sincerely yours . . .

119

Torre del Lago
November 13, 1914

Dear Adami,

Stanzas received! They are *almost* what I want. If necessary, we shall correct (what a very inappropriate word!) them at your convenience.

Life is *running on* fairly well. I am working. Let me remind you of the third act. May it be as God decrees and the humble subscriber desires!

I am getting some good shooting. We are having perfectly splendid weather—wonderful sunshine. The new Lancia goes so well that it brings tears to my eyes (with its speed!). *I even go to Viareggio.* All's well.

Remember me to Signora Amalia and to Nené.

Affectionately yours . . .

120

Torre del Lago
November 18, 1914

My dear Adami,

Well, I have read and thoroughly considered the act. It is *thin*—that is its great fault. The general effect is poor, and it is too much like a comedy. I have some ideas. I see how it can be saved, but I do not wish to explain it all in writing even if I could. It is a thing that must be described and carried out when we meet. I think that we must create some new situation, some friction caused by the unwelcome appearance of Rambaldo. I am not very much attracted by this idea, but I think that he ought to appear in the third act—if for nothing else than to break the monotony. What do you think of a quarrel between the poet and Ruggero? My ideas are not definite enough to write down, but I could suggest many small points of departure and feel that if we could meet, these would only have to be mentioned before you would seize upon and make use of them with your accustomed sureness and clear vision. As it is, although I hate to tell you so, it will not do. The end must come more rapidly, after the violent scene of the letter—not a telegram, because telegrams, besides being too unmusical, are read in the telegraph office and matters as serious as that are not telegraphed. But that is a detail. Then I insist on its being the *February* carnival. Good-bye, swallows! We shall just have to let the *aria* go. I shall get ahead, then, with my work on Act II, which is almost ready; then we shall meet either here or at Milan, and as fast as four and four make eight we shall bring Act III to an end as we did Act II.

Kind regards.

121

> *Torre del Lago*
> *November 19, 1914*

Dear Adami,

I am utterly discouraged! That third act is tormenting me to such a horrible degree that perhaps *La Rondine* will remain, with its two acts only, to be published after the death of the composer. The plot won't do—it doesn't convince me. Where did he find Magda? In a convent perhaps? And so this great love of his dies in an instant as soon as he learns who she is? Anyone who sees and hears such a drama unfolded must remain unconvinced and find the end almost illogical and quite unreal. And when the public is not convinced there isn't a shred of hope for the opera. I am in despair. Even the second act is rather dead. All that crowd of thoughtless revellers say very little, and we nowhere arrive at one of those moments of mad folly which are characteristic of such evenings or nights in the *cafés* of Paris. But Act III in its present state is quite useless, quite dead. Just the usual duet and an end which violates reason and carries no conviction. What is to be done? Is there any solution?

I can send the contract back to Vienna and start thinking of something else. Believe me, dear Adami, my eyes are wide open and—*La Rondine* is a solemn piece of stupidity. I curse the day when I made a contract with Vienna.

Affectionately yours . . .

[198]

122

> *Milan*
> *February 24, 1915*

Dear Adami,

The quartet is driving me mad. I cannot fit in the words of that tiresome pair, the poet and the girl. We must just sit down at the table together and in a good half hour's work settle those words. Tomorrow at five? Does that suit you?

Kindest regards.

123

> *Torre del Lago*

Dear Adami,

I need lines in the metre of the quartet for Magda, who at present says only, *"Sì, t'ascolto che paura."*[1] I must have other three lines, and then others for Lisetta and Prunier. That is, I want four quatrains, one for each: Magda: *Io sono L'ignota del bosco*[2] (four lines); Rug.: *No, sei la gioia,*[3] etc.; then four lines for Lisette and four for Prunier. The rest will do.

Sincerely . . .

---

[1] These lines do not appear in the final version.—TRANSLATOR.
[2] "I am the unknown one of the woods."
[3] "No, you are the joy . . ."

124

> *Torre del Lago*
> *March 11, 1915, Evening*

Dear Adami,

My solitude is vast like the sea, flat as the surface of a lake, black like night, and green as bile! My present indecision weakens and exhausts, stuns, and crushes me. Has Verona called you up as a conscript? I hope not. I am becoming as void of intelligence as a dumb rock growing grey under the ravages of time. The swallows fly unceasingly, and mine[1] makes me as restless as they. The Austrians have my crown, and I am crownless. I am like a king of cards. Music? I have no answer. To the winds, to the winds, like the ashes of suicides. Ricordi's proposals are degrading![2] In short, things simply can't go on like this. I am alone. Imagine how amusing it is! Nicche[3] is gone, called up. Tonio is in Milan. Write to me! I do not say come, because I know that you cannot. But if you were free what pleasure it would give me!

> Kindest regards . . .

[1] *I.e., La Rondine.*

[2] The contract with Vienna was by this time broken. Puccini did not accept Ricordi's terms and *La Rondine* was published by Sonzogno. This is the only break in Puccini's long and very friendly connection with the house of Ricordi.—TRANSLATOR.

[3] Nicche was Puccini's attendant on his fowling expeditions. He is still living at Torre del Lago, now, alas, keeper of Puccini's tomb.

125

Torre del Lago
August 22, 1915

Dear Adamino,
 I feel that with Tito things are not going well for *La Rondine*. Well, it can't be helped. I shall try to make different conditions for different countries, especially as this also suits my own desire in the matter. But after that? I shall try to conclude some arrangement in London, since I cannot in Italy. And certainly I can't give this opera away for nothing.
 I can see that Tito has no faith in it. Perhaps he will be sorry yet. Because if the subject is merely pleasant, I at least think that the music has some value. Perhaps I am mistaken—and I shall not insist. I have said it too often already. The third act is nearing the end and is very good. I have taken out all that dramatic stuff, and the end is approached quietly and delicately without any orchestral blaring or screaming. It is all in keeping.
 I shall arrive on the night of the twenty-sixth with the midnight train *via* Genoa.
 Kind regards to your wife and little one and to you, my dear friend.

126

> *Torre del Lago*
> *September 27, 1915*

Dear Adamino,

I want the old libretto of Act III of *La Rondine*, because I should like to see the first version of the scene of the reproaches. What he says in this version seems to me more effective and more convincing. That *passing over* the past is a human thing. Ruggero, in short, mustn't be a blockhead at all for not having seen that Magda was not an early violet.

> Yours ever . . .

127

> *Torre del Lago*

Dear Adamino,

I am going to Monsummano for about a week. Then I shall come back here. That for your guidance. I have the idea—and will you think about it too? —of making an entire change in the scene of Lisette and Prunier in Act III. You can be preparing it in the meantime. I should suggest that we make the two arrive on the scene to tempt Magda (seduction trio). Magda is very much upset at their departure (they have come specially to take her away from there), and when Ruggero comes in with his mother's letter she decides to go away.

Take out the *Chi sei, che hai fatto?*[1] with the *contaminata* [smirched] which follows—*i.e.*, all that dramatic stuff that is there now. There is not very much to change, in fact, in this act. It just wants to be lightened a bit and brought more into keeping with the kind of opera it is meant to be. The trio too must have some light, amusing touches.

Good-bye.

Yours affectionately . . .

I should lighten, *i.e.*, shorten, the whole scene also of the tea. It is too wordy, and some of it is unnecessary. In the first act I should leave out the scene of the mistake and put the tenor's *romanzetta* at the point where Rambaldo asks him, *È la prima volta che venite a Parigi?*"[2] The *romanzetta* there; and then as a result let the hand-reading scene be short.

128

Torre del Lago

Dear Adami,
I am here with no work to do. Think of it! What can I do? *La Houppelande*[3] must be done over again. I can do nothing to *La Rondine* without you. Think about it and don't abandon me like this. Come

---

[1] "Who are you? What have you done?"
[2] "Is this the first time that you have come to Paris?"
[3] Giuseppe Adami was at this time engaged on the libretto for *Il Tabarro* (*The Cloak*), adapted from Didier Gold's one-act play, *La Houppelande.*—TRANSLATOR.

then. I shall expect you on the 10th. Hurry up with your play—and good luck to you—and take the train for Torre. I should like to work, but cannot, since I have nowhere to put my notes. Bring the French original of *Il Tabarro*. We shall reread it together, and I believe that the drama will then take on a different aspect. As it stands it seems to me not only weak, but full of useless details. So come inspired with the desire to help me, and we shall soon finish it.

Kind regards to you and your wife.

Yours affectionately . . .

Friday midnight

Work your hardest.

129

Torre del Lago

Dear Adami,

It is beastly weather. I haven't a spark of energy. Elvira is ill, but a bit better now. Tonio was here last night and has just gone. Carignani is scratching away at the arrangement for piano, and I am vomiting over the score. Nothing from Vienna. We need an *aria* for Prunier, something in keeping with his character (with a better beginning) at the moment when Lisette re-enters Magda's service. Prunier must say something to Magda about it. This is essential. Otherwise this character, who is more or less the philosopher of the piece, would cut a sorry figure as nothing better than the follower of the maid-servant. This will not do. He must find an opportunity of saying to Magda, "I must speak to you," and he could say this when Lisette goes out for the white apron. Then Prunier can say, "My dear, I *know* that *he* wants to marry you, and that is impossible. You were not born to live cooped up in Montauban." And with that he begins to mock at the old woman and the house and the kind of life they represent. Then he goes on: "You can guess: this youth," etc., etc. Do you understand? *This is necessary.* Prunier must not play so mean a part at the end. This can be fitted in quite well and it is a case for something special.

Recitative: "You were not born for this. Your life is in Paris and you are ruining yourself."

Aria: "The absurdities of Montauban," etc., etc.

Please send me an answer quickly. What do you think?

130

Saturday, Holy Week, 1916

Dear Adami,

La Rondine is absolutely finished! I think the last scene is very good.

I am orchestrating *Il Tabarro*.[1]

I have given up composition for the moment, because we shall have to revise the libretto in two or three places where it lacks character.

[1] *The Cloak*, from Didier Gold's play, *La Houppelande.*—TRANSLATOR.

Have you nothing new in the way of subjects? I can find nothing! It is desperate! I search and search. I thought I had found two acts but they have come to nothing.

All good wishes from
Yours affectionately . . .

131

Torre del Lago
March 3, 1918

Dear Adami,

Thank you for the passage to insert, which is very good. I am disturbed by your letter. I understand your doubts and your anxiety about Paris. I do not know how to advise you at this stage. Certainly if you are not sure at the rehearsals it would be better to revise. . . . Of course, if you could keep calm the author ought to be the best judge, but we artists are never calm when we are approaching the ordeal.

Poor Signora Giuditta![1] I shall come to Milan.

The duet at the end makes Act III stronger. Good. People went mad over *Butterfly* at Pisa. I am invited to-morrow to the usual celebrations—what a treat!!!

Cheer up. I wish you courage and good luck.

Yours affectionately . . .

[1] Giuditta, the wife of Giulio Ricordi, had just died.

132

> *Torre del Lago*
> *31, or rather August 1, 1919*

Dear Adami,

I leave tomorrow. I was trying tonight—at the piano—to compose a trio for the third act. My idea was to ridicule the dullness of Montauban and recall the little *motif* of *Se sapessi ballar*[1] of Act II. This trio must be the climax of Act III. Don't forget that I want it arranged in short stanzas.

Write to me at Montecatini Alto. . . .

Yours affectionately . . .

133

> *Grosseto*
> *October 18, 1919*

Dear Adami,

The act has arrived. Farinelli writes me that they will have the new scenes made by Caramba, because Brunelleschi is in Paris, and they can do nothing without Renzo. And so it's the same story over again!

Why is it that I never get what I want? But I do insist that *La Rondine* should have new scenery.

I am glad that you and Simoni are considering a subject for me. Let it be passionate, moving, and at the same time not of vast, but of varied scope.

[1] "If I knew how to dance."

Remember that I have absolutely no work to do and that I need work to live by, for material food isn't enough for me. Tell Simoni that I shall expect him at Torre della Tagliata. You will come together to enjoy the delights of our ancient Greece. You will be staggered by the beauty of the place.

There will be everything that you two can desire! You will find Bordeaux of 1904 and grapes from Lecce; tobacco from Brazil, and Abdullah cigarettes. Boats, motor-launches, motor-bicycles, every kind of tackle for fishing, everything you want for fowling.

Good-bye, dear Adamino; if I get a good new subject I think that I shall do you honour, if you have any need of that. . . .

Yours affectionately . . .

134

Torre del Lago
November 14, 1919

Dear Adami,

Thank you for your delightful letter, sparkling with hope. Have you seen Renzo? What about Brunelleschi? Is he coming, will he come, will he do it?

Sonzogno writes me that Mocchi would like to give *La Rondine* in December at the Verdi Theatre in Florence with della Rizza, but he wants to use the Colon scenery.[1] I have replied that I am pleased with the protagonist, but

[1] *I.e.*, the scenery used in the production of *La Rondine* in the Colon Theatre in Buenos Aires.—TRANSLATOR.

cannot yet decide about the rest—because with the old scenes it is not satisfactory, especially in the third act, where a kind of short *intermezzo* is needed.

Go to Sonzogno and explain the second and third acts to him.

When am I to have the pleasure of knowing something about your new creation? Why not tell me at least where the scene is laid and the time? You ask too much of me: to judge everything all at once. When I get to know a subject gradually I become attached to it and absorbed in it, and the business of judging is accompanied by less surprise. Theatrecraft, if it is to be sound and to live, is so terribly difficult. I trust, however, in the collaboration of two gifted young men who are fully aware of the difficulties, and I await the result with confidence.

Affectionately yours . . .

135

Torre del Lago
July 9, 1920

Dear Adamino,

I am just back from the Maremma and found your letter awaiting me. I am waiting now for the result of your labours, and I pray God that the second and third acts will be as good as the first. What are you doing in Milan? Are there no directors in Ricordi's at present? Valcarenghi is in Paris, I know, but Clausetti ——? Please send me a card at once.

We are simply boiled here. I should like to go away, but need something to push me. My health is good, but my life useless without work.

Tell me what you are doing besides *Turandot*. Any plays? What's doing in Milan? Go to Sonzogno's and tell them that they ought not to have destroyed the first edition of *La Rondine*.[1]

When I was in Paris on my way home from London I found everybody at the Opéra-Comique in love with *La Rondine*, which they had heard at Monte Carlo. They would like to give it in Paris, but they are afraid of being *shot* because I monopolise the theatre too much and have the great defect (*sic*) of making too much *argent*!

Ask if the first edition is really still in existence or not. I could make an agreement with London too, but will the firm undertake the French and English translations? Every good wish to you and Signora Amalia, Nené, and your baby girl. My greetings to our friend Renato, who I hope will come to the Maremma in December.

136

Torre del Lago
December 3, 1920

Dear Adamino,

On Saturday I hope to leave for the Maremma. As soon as I have settled in there I shall write, or, better, wire to you to come. Then please let me know

---

[1] This was not, in fact, destroyed.—TRANSLATOR.

in good time, a few days before. Try to arrive by the morning train or in the evening by the one due at something after six: *consult the timetable.* Your station is Orbetello, and from there to the jungle it is about five miles—by infernal roads—but when you are there it is either suicide or bliss unalloyed. There is no middle way. Well, that is settled. Bring me the orchestra score of *La Rondine,* first edition, and some copies of the libretto. I have the piano arrangement here. It will be better if you send a telegram too. Send it to Orbetello, just two days before you are coming.

Yours affectionately . . .

IX

Il Trittico

AFTER *La Fanciulla del West*, Puccini for long could find no libretto which interested him, and he then conceived the idea of composing three one-act operas, hoping that it would be easier, even if it meant applying to three different authors, to obtain subjects.

Many projects were abandoned in this period, chief of them all being *The Children's Crusade*, in collaboration with Gabriele d'Annunzio.

At last, in the spring of 1912, Puccini seemed definitely to have found a subject. He had been greatly interested and attracted by the Quintero brothers' *Anima Allegra*, and, with the help and encouragement of Giulio Ricordi, Giuseppe Adami adapted the play and wrote the verses for all three acts. This was the last collaboration of Giulio Ricordi with Giacomo Puccini. The great publisher, who had loved Puccini like a father and had constantly inspired him with his affectionate and valuable counsels, closed in that year his long and distinguished career.

For reasons which we shall see later, when we speak of the various libretti which were not set to music, Puccini abandoned the idea of *Anima Allegra* completely a few years after the death of Giulio Ricordi.

Some one told him of a one-act play which had been

produced in Paris, *La Houppelande*,[1] by Didier Gold. Puccini went to see it. He liked the play, especially for its atmosphere, the setting so full of colour, of the Seine, and the wandering life of the bargemen. These, if treated and developed well in a libretto, seemed likely to provide good musical material. And so it came about that within a few days the scenario was drawn up, and Puccini, if only to put an end to his idleness, began to write the music.

Two other subjects would no doubt appear from somewhere to complete the trilogy. It was in this period, however, in 1914, that *La Rondine* came definitely into existence as a subject, and *Il Tabarro*, although almost completed, was set aside.

Some years after, in 1917, the idea of *Il Trittico*[2] began to materialise. Giovacchino Forzano had submitted to Puccini the plot of *Gianni Schicchi*. Puccini was charmed with it. This very fine libretto was a success at the first reading. So that was the third opera, and a good one! Now only the middle one was wanting. It was Forzano again who conceived and wrote the exquisitely delicate *Suor Angelica*, the mystical subject of which Puccini had so long dreamed. Within two months, without effort or uncertainty, I might almost venture to say without work, these two acts were set to music. It remained only to spend a few days finishing *Il Tabarro*, and the three one-act operas were ready for their great adventure. A curious

[1] *The Cloak*, which became Puccini's *Il Tabarro.*—TRANSLATOR.
[2] The word *trittico* is properly used in Italian, as "triptych" in English, to denote a picture divided into three parts or painted on three folding panels.—TRANSLATOR.

episode in the history of *Suor Angelica* was the audition which the composer gave of it in the convent of Vico-pelago near Lucca, where his eldest sister was a nun in an enclosed order.

Puccini was greatly moved when he told the story of this performance. The little nuns stood round, absorbed, breathless with attention. His sister turned the pages for him, while Giacomo played and explained the words of the songs to them. Phase by phase, the opening episodes of the novices with their mistress and the monitor, the little scene of the wishes,[1] and then the strange secret sadness of Sister Angelica, had interested and enthralled them. It may be that each of the listeners found in that music something of her own heart. When he reached the scene of the princess aunt, Puccini stopped in embarrassment. He had to explain the heroine's story, had to tell them of her past and the sin of love which had stained her fair fame, and of that son who had been taken away from her and whose death was now brutally announced. And there was worse to come. He had to tell them of the despairing suicide and the divine pardon of the miracle.

"It was not easy," said Puccini. "Still, with as much tact and skill as I could summon, I explained it all. I saw many eyes that looked at me through tears. And when I came to the *aria, Madonna, Madonna, salvami per amor di mio figlio!*[2] all the little nuns cried, with voices full of pity but firm in their decision, 'Yes, yes, poor things!' "

[1] Where Sister Angelica sings *"I desideri sono i fior dei vivi"* ("Wishes are the flowers of the living").—TRANSLATOR.
[2] "Save my soul for love of my son."

And so with human compassion and Christian charity the real nuns absolved their phantom sister.

Il Trittico was performed for the first time at the Costanzi in Rome on the night of January 11, 1919.[1] Public and critics were unanimous in its praise. After *Il Tabarro* the King sent for Puccini and had a long and very friendly conversation with him in the royal box.

The principal singers in the three operas were Maria Labia, the tenor, Di Giovanni, Galeffi, the baritone in *Il Tabarro*, Della Rizza, protagonist in *Suor Angelica*, and Galeffi again as protagonist in *Gianni Schicchi*.

In the following season *Il Trittico* was given with tremendous success in the Metropolitan Theatre in New York and afterwards in the principal theatres of Italy and the rest of Europe.

But the success of the three operas together was short lived. For some years now the tendency has been to separate the three members of the trilogy. Of the three in their separate performances the most successful has been *Gianni Schicchi*.

(The letters in this section were all addressed to Adami.)

[1] This was the first performance in Italy. It was, in fact, first produced at the Metropolitan Theatre in New York in November, 1918.—TRANSLATOR.

137

Torre del Lago
October 23, 1915

Dear Adamino,

I have set to work in the meantime on *La Houppelande*. Are you prepared to go over the libretto with me again? I think that if you were here we could settle everything within a week. You could also finish *La Rondine*, and we could tackle seriously the question of *Gli Zoccoletti*.[1] And we'd settle especially the problem of the third act. I am promising myself again to finish *Il Tabarro* in a few weeks, and I think that it will be good. From the point of view of contrast, too, I think that it suits me better just now than *Gli Zoccoletti*.

Write to me if you will, can, and want to come here for some days.

Affectionately yours . . .

138

Torre del Lago

Dear Adamino,

Here I am back again from the strange and fascinating Maremma. A wild and primitive country, far, far away from the world; where the spirit really finds rest and the body strength (in winter only). I have had

---

[1] The title of the projected opera on the subject of Ouida's *Two Little Wooden Shoes.*—TRANSLATOR.

a great time snipe-shooting and roaming through these wild woods.

So I hear that you are putting off the comedy for a bit? It isn't a bad idea, especially as you will give it at Lent reconsidered and repolished (if it needed that) and you are its best judge. I am working a little on *Il Tabarro*. I have written the *finale* of the river song. But (groans from Adami) I need more lines. It is too short at present. Affectionate greetings to you all from

Yours . . .

We shall meet at Christmas.

139

Torre del Lago
Wednesday

Dear Adamino,

Tonio tells me that the lines are coming for the end of the duet for soprano and baritone. I have written the music up to the words *trascinate dall'onda*.[1] Here I wanted a passionate interruption from Giorgetta: two lines or even one hendecasyllable. Then my idea was to make cuts so as to reach the end—*i.e.*, the *resta vicina a me, la notte è bella*[2] more quickly. I should like to cut from *le soste sotto i salici* to *notti di estate* and get straight to the end. What do you think? Then I must *absolutely* have the last two lines of the *sobborgo* duet—

[1] "Swept away by the tide."
[2] "Stay here beside me, the night is beautiful."

Parigi che ci guarda e che compensa la nostra povertà con tutti i sogni.[1] They do not seem to me the inspired lines one needs for the end of a scene.

I beseech you, therefore, *with feet and hands clasped*, to put some warmth into them and give me a wingèd end, or if you can't find wings, at least make it effective, as an end should be.

Regards to you and to your wife and Nené.

140

Torre del Lago
May 2, 1916

Dear Adamino,

I have orchestrated everything as far as I have composed the music. I have finished, therefore, a good half of *Il Tabarro*. It has turned out well—I am more than satisfied with it. Now for the rest! But I shall require a good many changes. Meanwhile I shall set to work on the duet between Giorgetta and Michele, which is what I wanted. Then we shall arrange to meet.

Give me some news of yourself. Kindest regards to you all.

[1] "Paris that watches over us and compensates our poverty with all her dreams."

141

> *Torre del Lago*
> *May 29, 1916*

Dear Adamino,

Tito is in Paris and writes me asking if the changes are to my liking. I have written to say yes, and, in fact, as I said in my telegram to you, they are very good indeed. But you must seriously think of another subject. This is a gadfly that stings me continually. But, for all my thinking and all my scrutiny of my thoughts of today and yesterday, nothing emerges that is of any use to me. It is sad, very sad, for time is flying. . . .

I was expecting a letter from you, as you promised. Regards to you and your wife and little boy.

142

> *Torre del Lago*
> *June 14, 1916*

Dear Adami,

First of all, have you a copy of the libretto of *Il Tabarro?* I hope so. Well, in the duet between Giorg. and Mich., p. 23, at *resta vicina a me* . . . *non ti ricordi*[1] I find myself compelled to make the baritone go on singing in a languid sort of way, while Giorgetta remains silent, with hardly an interruption. So that it is not really a duet, and then there is the river monologue soon after.

[1] "Stay here close to me . . . don't you remember."

[219]

This is all for the baritone, and it is too much. *Ergo*, I want you to make this second part of the supposed duet between Michele and Giorgetta into a real duet by means of interruptions from Giorgetta, and to make it livelier so as to escape the slow languor which spoils it at present. It can become affectionate and even despairing at the end, before the *S'invecchia*[1] of Giorgetta. I know that it is difficult to make her—the accused one—speak, but she must, in order to avoid an unbroken monotony which would injure the opera.

I hope that I have been clear.

Affectionately yours . . .

143

July 27, 1916

Dear Adami,

It is raining, thank God!

I received your alterations. Some are all right, some not. But it doesn't matter. They are little things that we shall put right in a quarter of an hour. Have you any ideas? I search and find none. And your plays? and life? What a miserable thing it is! These last months have been horrible! What a useless thing is art! But to us it is a necessity of both soul and body!

Affectionate regards to you all.

---

[1] "We're growing old."

144

> *Torre del Lago*
> *September 2* [*1916*]

Dear Adamino,

I am back again and attacking the orchestration of *Il Tabarro* (second half). We shall settle the words of the monologue afterwards. It is easier to work now because it is cooler. Are you doing anything interesting? Are you working?

About *La Rondine* I cannot yet tell you anything. *Il Tabarro* will be finished within a month. And afterwards? Have you nothing for me? No ideas, projects, plots? I have a tiny little idea of my own, but I am afraid that it will hardly stand on its feet. I shall tell you about it some time.

Affectionate greetings.

Regards to Tito: where is he?

145

> *Torre del Lago*
> *November 10, 1916*

Dear Adami,

It is true that I am lazy not to have written you, but I always meant to write, and that redeems me. Well, I am working—slowly and softly, but moving! I have now reached the duet between Michele and Giorgetta. I have, however, left Luigi and Giorgetta on one side; but I have orchestrated and arranged for piano everything up to the song of Frugola, which has still got a leg in the air. But I'll bring it down presently. The fact is that this opera is not an easy one, far from it. It will be finished before the autumn, and Tito writes me from Paris that he has said yes to Gunsbourg, of Monte Carlo, and I am pleased. A small theatre and a good general rehearsal.

Where are you going next summer? To Viareggio? No? Yet if you think it over it isn't such a bad place for a holiday.

Elvira is pretty well. She sends regards to you and your wife and Nené.

Yours affectionately . . .

146

Dear Adamino,

Thank you for your letter. Give Caramba my very best wishes—poor fellow!

I am working at the new nun. I think that you ought to hunt round and find three original and not dismal acts for me and my notes, because I am afraid that old Florence is not a subject that suits me or is so very attractive to the public outside Italy. You see, I write for all the races of men—including the negroes when they will have reached their full development! (What pretensions!)

Are you coming to Viareggio? I am hoping it so much!

If you would like me to find rooms for you. . . . But I warn you that this year the hotels are making preposterous charges.

About Ferraris for the Dal Verme, she is the very person I want. Suggest Georgesky for Prunier. Certainly it is rather difficult to find anybody else, but we mustn't give up hope.

I am well. I shall be better when I have my dear Adamino beside me.

Affectionately yours . . .

147

Paris

Dear Adami,

Schicchi went really well. Except for one or two artists not quite up to the mark, the *ensemble* is good, and then Marcoux is a great protagonist. Tonight Brunelleschi is coming to dinner with me, and I think that Tito will come too. Then tomorrow morning I leave at nine with the *de luxe* train and reach Pisa at nine on Friday.

Paris is beautiful, but it tires me. They are very kind to me. Last night after the performance I went to the Café de Paris, one of the most *chic* places, where I was very kindly received by everybody, including the *maîtres d'hôtel.* The orchestra played *Butterfly.* I had to get up and acknowledge it. In the shops, too, where I give my name they either ask for my autograph or line up to do me honour when I go out. In short, we are popular but . . . old.

Affectionate regards to you and your wife and everybody.

X

Libretti Not Set to Music

SIDE by side with those operas of Puccini's which will continue to live and to delight and move all the publics of the world, there is a series of projected operas, begun, and in some cases carried to a certain degree of elaboration, and then suddenly dropped. This abandonment, coming sometimes immediately after the first fervid illusions, shows that Puccini's infallible sense of the theatre never let itself be dazzled, and that amid alternations of hope and diffidence he knew how to maintain that solid equilibrium which rarely allowed him a mistake in the very difficult task of choosing a libretto.

The episode of Verga's *Lupa* is well known. The idea was conceived immediately after *Manon*. The Sicilian drama had attracted both the publisher and the still very young composer. Puccini felt that it would make a powerful opera, full of colour; and, with a view to studying this colour and concluding the negotiations already opened with Giovanni Verga, he was soon in Sicily. Everything seemed to be decided. The Sicilian author and the Tuscan composer had come to a complete agreement even on the details of the adaptation of the story as a libretto.

Then one day the composer took ship home again by way of Livorno. There were few passengers on board;

but there was a small piano; and there was also the Marchesa Gravina, Wagner's stepdaughter, child of Cosima Wagner by her first marriage with Bülow.

Puccini, hearing this, felt it his duty to open the little piano and draw from it the strains of *Tannhäuser*. Mutual introductions followed, and the two were soon friends and exchanging confidences.

Manon Lescaut . . . just had a triumphant success. . . . A certain and brilliant future. . . . The libretto? . . . Yes . . . Wagner wrote his own. . . . Lucky fellow! . . .

And now? What next? . . . *La Lupa?* . . . What, a Sicilian subject? A realistic drama? . . . H'm. . . . Is there a procession? . . . Yes, certainly, the procession for Good Friday. . . . *Dio mio!* Procession . . . priests . . . the crucifix. . . .

And then . . . she offered her advice: "No, listen, Maestro" . . . The ship sailed on. . . . Sicily faded out of sight. . . . *La Lupa* gradually crumbled. . . .

By the time Livorno appeared in the distance nothing was left of the Sicilian drama.

There was at one time a *Marie Antoinette* which Puccini liked very much. Illica had drawn up a vast scenario of it. There were thirteen or fourteen episodes, not definitely worked out, but sketched. Then began the work of collaboration with Puccini. It was rather a curious collaboration, because at each sitting the scenic material suffered more and more elimination, and within a month the scenes were reduced to eight.

"Don't you think it is more effective that way?"

And Illica, who willingly followed Puccini's advice, agreed.

But little by little, as their deliberations went on, the number of the scenes diminished still further; from eight to seven, seven to six, to five, to four, to three. Clearly, Illica was thinking:

"All right; when we come to three, we shall stop. After all, Puccini may well be right. A fine *Marie Antoinette* in three acts, with the last scene in the prison. . . . Why not?"

Alas! The prison remained, but even the other two scenes were gradually eliminated. It seems that by that time Illica could stand it no longer. All his researches, all his work and weary toil, gone for nothing, ruthlessly destroyed!

And one fine morning, at the end of his tether, he gave vent to his wrath to Giulio Ricordi. He inveighed against art, against Marie Antoinette, and against Puccini with the passionate vehemence known to all his friends. Giulio Ricordi, while recognising that Illica was not wholly in the wrong, acknowledged without a doubt that Puccini by this time had made an end of *Marie Antoinette*.

How many other projects shared with Illica were born, lived for a time, and died! There was a *Notre Dame*, for instance, which cost them whole months of useless labour; and a *Tartarin* on which they spent a long period of careful elaboration and for which Giacomo Puccini journeyed to Paris, and mounted the five flights of stairs to where Alphonse Daudet awaited him, already in the grip of the malady which was soon to carry him off. Puccini used to recall how the noble face, wasted by disease, lighted up with joy at the thought that his hero might live again in music.

He used to speak also of another visit, to Émile Zola, when after much hesitation he had finally decided to make an opera of *La Faute de l'Abbé Mouret*. Puccini himself sketched the first scenario for this opera.

With Maurice Maeterlinck, too, Puccini was very anxious to arrange something. Once, in fact, he had already quite decided for *Pelléas et Mélisande*. Here at last was the opera in scenes, for which he had long been searching, which had almost materialised in the famous *Marie Antoinette* and which was to turn up again long afterwards in the *Two Little Wooden Shoes*, another project almost realised and then, little by little, dropped.

Pelléas et Mélisande, then. There was no time to lose, and he was off on a journey to find Maeterlinck.

Proposal, answer, collapse of his plans!

"Alas! How willingly would I give my poem to the composer of *La Vie de Bohème* if I had not already given it to Debussy!"

Puccini had also thought of deriving a libretto from *La Femme et le pantin* of Pierre Louys.

Maurice Vaucaire was chosen to write the libretto, and from Paris he journeyed to Torre del Lago, where in little more than a month he gave shape to Puccini's idea of the story of Conchita.[1]

The libretto was ready. It had now to be put into verse. Maurice Vaucaire wrote the whole poem in French. The newspapers published interviews about it. *Conchita* was a splendid venture, the protagonist a magnificent type, and the opera rich in colour. Yes, but all the same. . . .

And then with the libretto completed, his doubts began, at first few and hesitating, then more numerous and more compelling.

And so *Conchita*, too, died.

Conchita died, as later died *Anima Allegra*, although its heroine knew none of the subtle cruelties of her perverted sister, but had so much poetry in her heart and such mad desire of the sunshine! So died many other fair dreams of which we find traces in these letters. There, for instance, we read of negotiations with Gabriele d'Annunzio, and of the long conversations at Arcachon when the idea was born first of *The Rose of Cyprus* and then of *The Children's Crusade*.

The poet had communicated all his own fervour to the composer. He had expounded his theme with such lucid clearness that Puccini parted from him convinced that he had found for his music a great poem. The arrival of the manuscript changed all that. Or, rather, it was the manuscript itself that had changed! D'Annunzio in the process of writing had created something entirely differ-

[1] The heroine of Pierre Louÿs' *La Femme et le pantin*. Puccini's opera was to be called *Conchita*.—TRANSLATOR.

ent from the verbal sketch which he had given to Puccini.

The letters which reflect these gropings and experiments deserve some space in such a collection as this, since they reveal how much toil and thought went to the final choice of a libretto.

148

To Luigi Illica[1]

Dear Illica,

I do not know where to turn with all this chopping and changing. If there is a great opera, a real, big, solid one, let it come and welcome, even if it should never leave the publisher's shelves. But to my mind, *Notre Dame* is certainly not that. There is not a breath of real or sincere poetry in it. I repeat that I would welcome the right subject! But this, alas, is not it. Look for it and choose something real, something sincere and convincing, even if it is slight.

Yours . . .

[1] The poet who collaborated with Giuseppe Giacosa in the libretti of *La Bohème, Tosca,* and *Madama Butterfly.*

149

To Giulio Ricordi

> *Torre del Lago*
> *February 18, 1906*

My dear Signor Giulio,
Here I am at Torre. I am well and await my *orders* to go to Nice. I had a conversation with the Poet,[1] and I think that he has good, sound ideas.

He will give me a theme created specially for music— a human drama in an exalted lyrical vein—three acts, interesting and moving—so he says.

Let's hope that we'll hit the mark this time. Meanwhile, however, I have not abandoned the idea of *La Femme et le pantin*—and I beg you to find out from the French Society of Authors if it is available or not.

150

To Giulio Ricordi

> *[Paris]*
> *Wednesday Night*

Dear Signor Giulio,
I have received Illica's material. It is far too different from his first sketch and Louÿs' novel.

Still, there are good things—very good things—in it.

[1] Probably d'Annunzio, to whom Puccini appears to refer when he writes *Poeta* with a capital.—TRANSLATOR.

Now, in order to settle things definitely, wouldn't it be a good thing if Illica were to come to Paris, and, with the help of Vaucaire, Pierre Louys, and your humble servant, pronounce *la dernière parole*? At our present distance from each other it is impossible to do anything satisfactorily.

I had lunch again today with Louys, and we *worked* at the libretto. He is so pleased that I am composing this opera and is so friendly. I believe that Illica's presence here would mean the practical completion of the libretto and at once!

Kindest regards.

Bohème is on again tonight, and all the seats are taken.

151

To Giulio Ricordi

Boscolungo Abetone
August 6, 1906

Dear Signor Giulio,

I went yesterday to Pietrasanta to see d'Annunzio, and he told me of a subject which seemed to me good. It is still rather in the clouds, I admit, but it has come down near enough to earth. It is rather romantic, of a type somewhere between legend and fairytale, with a tragic end. It has to be altered still and discussed. But it seems to me to lend itself to music, and it has good dramatic interest. The scene is laid in Cyprus in the days when the island flourished as a meeting-place of all nations.

D'Annunzio is coming to me here about the 15th with two acts written, and we shall see. It is a three-act opera with a short prologue.

From Vaucaire I have had six scenes, some good, some of no use. The *grille* scene is not a success. I am writing to him now. He, too, is coming about the 23rd. In short, the pot is boiling. I am very well. I am extremely sorry about your news of the Exhibition, but I hope that it will not be a great loss for you. The papers say nothing about it.

Kindest regards.

152

To Giulio Ricordi

Boscolungo Abetone
August 13, 1906

My dear Signor Giulio,
The news I am sending is by no means joyful, but I want to tell you that for the present the agreement with d'Annunzio has petered out. I revealed to him my doubts on a subject of his, and he wrote to me very courteously that he was sorry about my doubt and wished all success to the new music which I should compose! I telegraphed to him that I had no wish to renounce his collaboration and that we ought to meet again. Up to the present I have received no reply. I shall keep you in-

formed of everything, and I should like to tell you also what the subject was.

Affectionate greetings.

153

To Giulio Ricordi

Boscolungo Abetone
August 23, 1906

Dear Signor Giulio,
I wrote to you the other day about my disappointment with the Poet's libretto. I have heard no more, not even from Tito, who I believe has been to see him. Vaucaire has been here for a day or two and is working—and with good results. It is turning out very beautiful. Difficult, but, I think, convincing and original.

It is time to consider the choice of a translator. For *La Femme* we want a *strong, vigorous* poet, capable of sudden, daring flights, with courage in plenty and an abundance of shining colours on his palette. Who is there? I am doing my best, but cannot think of one. Meanwhile, even if it is only in French, we have the libretto.

All my affectionate greetings, and I hope that the cure has done you good.

154

To Giulio Ricordi

> *Paris*
> *November 14, 1906*

Dear Signor Giulio,
    I had already had telegrams from New York. Thanks also for yours. As for Illica, we are in a glorious mess! Pierre Louys and—I too—find Illica's proposals absolutely out of keeping with the subject. (We can leave Vaucaire out of the question. He is the most injured party, the most interested in protesting against Illica's ideas.[1])

Pierre Louys has chewed and discussed, digested and approved of, the plan and the separate scenes of the libretto, because he has found them flesh of his flesh, and words, thoughts, and details are all, whether obviously or not, his own.

Certainly he does not yet like the curtains, especially after the second scene and at the dance-*café*, and in this I agree with him.

And this was what we wanted Illica to do, instead of interfering with almost all the details and even some of the characters—like that of the mother, for instance.

I do not say that there were not some good theatrical ideas among Illica's proposals. He is too consummate a master of the theatre for that. But he does seem to me to

---

[1] Vaucaire had already completed the poem in French.—TRANSLATOR.

be leaving the track that was marked out for him and treading paths not made by the creator of the drama.

What do you advise me to do now? If Illica comes here and finds all this wind blowing against his ship? . . .

I shall wait for some advice from you: how and what am I to write to Illica so as to hurt him as little as possible? . . .

The rehearsals are going well here. The orchestra began this morning at last, *strings only*.

The stage rehearsals are proceeding under the scrupulous care of Carré. The opera will go on in the beginning of December.

Oscar Wilde's manuscript, *A Florentine Tragedy* (one act), which pleases me very much, has arrived. It is in English, however. I could have a good translation made here, a literary one, so as to get the full effect of Wilde's original. Tell me if I should have it done. It is only one act, but beautiful, inspired, strong, and tragic: three principal characters, three first-class *rôles*. Time, 1300. It would be a rival to *Salome*,[1] only more human, more real, and less alien from the feelings of everybody.

I should be grateful if you would write at once, both about the translation and about Illica.

Very many affectionate greetings from
Yours . . .

[1] The *Salome* of Richard Strauss, with libretto translated from another of Wilde's plays, had been produced at Dresden on December 9th, 1905.—TRANSLATOR.

155

To Giulio Ricordi

Torre del Lago
April 4, 1907

My dear Signor Giulio,
I am enjoying the rest and quiet, but my spirit is rebellious and wears itself out in the usual everlasting quest. I read and think and write: to Gorki, Matilde Serao, Belasco, and so on.

D'Annunzio is coming round again. I had a letter from him this morning saying that his "old nightingale has awakened with the spring and would gladly sing for me. . . ."

I receive schemes and libretti daily, all second-hand stuff. Colautti wants to find me the pearl of great price. (When you have seen *Gloria* would you please write me your opinion of its dramatic qualities?) To be frank with you, I find this life of inaction very irksome. I am conscious of so much creative force within me. And what can I do? Who will give me the subject that I need? My God, what a poor thing the theatrical world is, both here and abroad! But I'm not despairing. Faith will work the miracle. Write to me. I look forward to your letters and am delighted when they come.

If d'Annunzio does complete a libretto for me it will not mean that I am preparing nothing else. *La Femme* seems to me to have the elements of something very real and powerful.

Many affectionate greetings from
Yours . . .

[237]

156

To Giulio Ricordi

Torre del Lago
April 11, 1907

My dear Signor Giulio,
I did not answer your letter immediately because I confess it gave me a shock and left me feeling
rather unhappy. I have had the thought of writing to you
in my mind for some days, but have only now felt that
the moment has come. I reread your letter today, and
the impression is different. I see in it how much affection
you have for me and how great is your interest in one
who has always regarded you with feelings of the greatest trust and deference, joined with an unchanging
affection.

It would take a long time to thrash out the reasons
which have so poisoned the thought of *Conchita* as to
make me wish to abandon it.

It was not *fear* (confound the word!) of the *prudery*
of the Anglo-Saxon audiences of Europe and America.
It was not the example of *Salome* in New York.[1]

My reasons are based on practical and theatrical con-
siderations.

If I had had any preoccupation (I will not call it fear)
it would have been the thought of the musical colour and
brilliance of *Carmen*[2]—the one and only point on which

---

[1] *Salome* scandalised the New York public, and was withdrawn after one
performance in the Metropolitan Theatre (1907).—TRANSLATOR.

[2] *Conchita*, like *Carmen*, was a Spanish subject.—TRANSLATOR.

any composer would be reasonably bound to concern himself. I have devoted long hours of consideration to this subject. I have examined it as a spectator as well as a composer of opera, and I have come to the conclusion that the character of Conchita cannot be made clear to the spectator unless he has read the novel.

Then there are the different phrases of the strange and continuous dialogue so often repeated (five—no, six—duets), and forming one single situation which has one single subject—*the woman and the puppet*, or the approach of Conchita to Matteo and her withdrawal. Then I consider the final scene as it is in the novel (I am not thinking of the brutal part) quite impossible of performance, or, at least, of acceptance on the stage unless one is going to give the theatre a spectacle so *nature* that Aretino[1] himself wouldn't have dared to do it. And note that there is no other way of dealing with this *finale*.

There is also the difficulty of there being no baritone; and there is the problem as to why Morenito is with Conchita in the *grille* scene, and the certainty that all the audience will consider her to be what she is not. And what of the final proof of her virginity, the crux of the whole opera? How is it to be made clear to the audience that she has given herself, pure, for the first time and that all the appearances are false?

I do not deny that Louÿs' tale attracts me very much. Perhaps we ought to have departed somewhat from the novel, or at least have given it some different treatment

[1] Pietro Aretino, licentious poet and playwright of the sixteenth century.— TRANSLATOR.

which might have made it clearer to the public. Thus perhaps other situations would have arisen, other variations, other episodes, which would have relieved the monotony which is apparent in it now.

Besides, with discussion we could have found other ways. But this we did not have, since we were deprived of the help of the great counsellor who refused at the time to hear anything about this subject.

Vaucaire brought me a Conchita *tout à fait française* and devoid of any original character. It was I who set the poet on the right track again, and so perhaps we followed the novel too closely instead of using our imagination a little more.

I know, too, from experience that at other times, with other subjects, and amid alternations of despair and triumph we have succeeded in building upon varied, logical, and solid foundations works which are now alive and flourishing.

To conclude, I shall be in Milan soon, within two weeks at the latest. It is *by doctor's orders* that I do not come at once.

We shall then talk freely and calmly, and with complete confidence on both sides; and we shall have the discussion which I feel this work has missed. And then we shall read the beautiful translation,[1] and the reading will serve also to introduce to me a poet and perhaps a librettist, such a rare plant, almost undiscoverable in these days.

All my most affectionate greetings.

[1] This is probably the translation of *A Florentine Tragedy*, proposed in Letter 154.—TRANSLATOR.

157

To Giulio Ricordi

November 27, 1907

My dear Signor Giulio,
Illica came immediately on my summons. He has been here for some days, entirely given up to the work, which is making excellent progress, without any important departure from the old libretto.

He too is convinced about this new kind of opera which I have decided to write, and I hope when I come to Milan to convince you too.

Not an hour passes but we remember our Signor Giulio. I assure you that Illica is the same as of old, and that his feelings towards you are of the most affectionate. He deplores only that the suggestion of his having a collaborator should have been made by Signor Giulio and not by Franchetti, and in this too I sympathise with Illica, because after the success of *Germania*[1] it seems to me that Franchetti should not have made this proposal to Illica—and much less should you.

But, as you see, it is not a serious or irremediable wrong. It is best to ignore the pettinesses and gossip, etc., which spring up continually. The world is so false and cruel! For my part, therefore, I send my best wishes and beg all parties to return to the *stagion fiorita*, which was marked of old by such enthusiasm.

I am sending you three rather bad photographs. I have

---

[1] *Germania*, an opera by Alberto Franchetti, libretto by Luigi Illica. It was produced at Milan on March 11, 1902.

given orders for other, better, and larger, ones. All good wishes from us and from Illica.

158

To Tito Ricordi

Paris

Dear Tito,

Hardly any news. Tristan Bernard will try to find something else, but has not abandoned the *Ogre.* I have pointed out to him the likeness it bears to *Hänsel and Gretel.* He asked for the libretto, and I have this morning dispatched a copy to him. The other subject of which we have spoken is an African story, with an explorer in it.

Julien[1]*?* A chaos of bad taste: no action and such commonplace music. No feeling in it at all.

D'Annunzio tells me that he will make or find a noble subject for a one-act opera. But how can one lump him in one performance with other—unknown—names? He is willing to join with Tristan, and he thinks him a likely person to give me what I want. However, we parted with the understanding that he would consider the whole matter. He brought the *Crusade* up again, but I told him that for the present I could not abandon my own idea of three scenes. I let my tongue run on in a survey of my ideas of the Crusade. I thought that he was rather pleased

---

[1] Gustave Charpentier's opera which followed and forms a sequel to *Louise.*

with them. In *La Pisanella*, too, he has removed the scene of the crown on the cropped hair, which I had criticised at once when he described the *Rose of Cyprus* to me in the villa at Viareggio.

Gatti, to whom I wrote a resentful letter, wires me from Berlin, "Regrettable misunderstanding; *Fanciulla* remaining in our repertory." So that is all right.

On Thursday I shall be at the performance of *Butterfly*. I leave on Friday for London. I went to hear the *Sacre de Printemps*[1]: the choreography is ridiculous, the music sheer cacophony. There is some originality, however, and a certain amount of talent. But taken altogether, it might be the creation of a madman. The public hissed, laughed, and . . . applauded.

Yours ever . . .

159

To Carlo Marsilli

[Paris]
Friday Evening, 6 o'clock

Dear Carlino,[2]

I am leaving tomorrow night, Saturday. I've been in Paris more than a month now. I have fixed up for the other two operas with T. Bernard and d'Annunzio. I hope that they will materialise, so that I may have work for some time to come.

[1] A ballet by Stravinsky.—TRANSLATOR.
[2] Carlo Marsilli, an advocate, was Puccini's nephew.—TRANSLATOR.

[243]

Forzano writes me that he has been working. Good—
we shall see.

Greetings to you all.

160

To Giulio Ricordi

Dear Signor Giulio,
I have given much thought to *Anima Allegra*,
and think that I have contrived three good acts. It will
all, however, require to be done on a larger scale, enriched, and made more weighty as regards both characters and events. I am not going to tell you now how
I envisage the subject, because it would take too long
to describe it. I should say keep Adami and associate
Zangarini with him. I should not like to leave him out
of it. He defers to me and is fond of me, and since I shall
be the director of all the operations, I shall make the
two librettists vassals to my Doge. I have been pondering
this subject well in the last two days, and I firmly believe
that it will turn out a good and beautiful thing.

Three acts of different character:

ACT I. A large, imposing room.

ACT II. A piazza with a tattered tent belonging to some
gipsies, and a little church with whatever sort of campa-
nile can be managed. The act to finish with the girl ringing lengthily for the gipsy wedding which she has
sponsored, while the couple and procession enter or

leave the church—if it will be possible to have the marriage in the church; and this we shall see.

ACT III. Courtyard or large "patio" with final scene of flowers and conversion to merriment of all the croakers. The old woman must become the maddest of them all!! I see that I am beginning to be indiscreet about my own ideas. We shall talk about them later. Will you speak to Adami or wait till I come?

Very many affectionate greetings.

161

To Giulio Ricordi

Dear Signor Giulio,

You are right about postponing the choice of poets. Because besides the good writer of verses we must find the man who will bring to the subject his own contribution of merry and original fantasy. The comedy needs working out in many places, and the second act (of which I have just a glimmer of an idea) must be lively, amusing, and logical. I think and think and cannot find the man we need for this (or any other) type of play. Illica, for instance, has the right manner; he has superabundant fantasy which outweighs everything else, but is very sensitive about its being cut down and selected. Whom then shall we find? I should be glad to know if you have made any agreement with Adami.

Meanwhile, I am thinking and already have some

passable ideas. In the hope of seeing you soon—*i.e.*, after Genoa.

Many affectionate greetings from

Yours . . .

162

To Giulio Ricordi

Torre del Lago
March 22, 1912

Dear Signor Giulio,

Adami, having accomplished a first act in this Eden, carried it to the Almighty Father for judgment. He examined it and said, *"E va!"*[1]

Thus was born a woman whose name shall be *Anima Allegra*.

Do you think it would be fairer or more propitious to leave Adami in peace to finish his work as quickly as he can, or to send for examination by the *notary*[2] the act already completed?

I am on the point of departure for Carlomonte[3] immediately after the first night of my foreign *Girl*.

Wherever is Tito? The wretch never answers my letters!

Affectionate greetings.

[1] "It is good." There is, of course, a pun on the name Eve.—TRANSLATOR.
[2] *I.e.*, Giulio Ricordi.—TRANSLATOR.
[3] Monte Carlo (?).—TRANSLATOR.

163

To Giuseppe Adami

> *Torre del Lago*
> *Wednesday*

My *dear Adami,*
Thank you for the translations of Heine.
They are good. I like the poems so much for their delicate and original thought. The translations seem to me
to be very successful; if only they could have caught the
rhythm of the originals, but this would be too much
to ask.

I am still in great doubt about *Anima*, and in this
doubt my days pass very gloomily.

If only I could find *my subject*, a subject full of passion and pain! But time is passing, and it is my best
time!

> Affectionately yours . . .

164

To Giuseppe Adami

> *Torre del Lago*
> *September 30, 1912*

My *dear Adami,*
I am tossed on a sea of indecision, and in
consequence even *Anima Allegra* is a little island which

is still always within reach . . . and that is why I wrote to you to send me the libretto.

I came back here today, and I shall reread the libretto tomorrow . . . or when I have settled down, which will be in a few days. The idea of deserting Spain and transferring it to Holland seems good enough at first sight, but you are thus doing away with the original background from which emerge the types and customs entering into the play. Don't you think so?

I want you to give it all a good cleaning up, but to do this you must throw off the bonds of your four acts and really get down to the work of revision of both the form and the details of the action, especially in Act II.

That is all I have to say.

Every good wish from

Yours . . .

165

To Carlo Clausetti[1]

Via Verdi, 4
Milan
January 24, 1913

Dear Carlino,

I am afraid that I shall never come to an agreement now with d'Annunzio!

I shall try to go to Arcachon soon, about the beginning of February, as I have ideas about the *Crusade.* But he

[1] One of the present directors of the firm of Ricordi.

[248]

will probably not be able nor willing to accept them. I am a bit off colour. It is the fog—it is Milan, and all the struggle; in fact, I get more rest and feel better on the Tirreno.[1]

Yours ever . . .

166

To Giuseppe Adami

Torre del Lago
September 17, 1913

Dear Adami,

I have here the English comedy *Mollie*, which was produced at the Filo[2] by Emma Gramatica, and which I like very much. I have got hold of it by a secret channel. I think that one could make a delightful opera of it.

Do you know it? And do you think that you could make a scenario of it and write the verse? Let me know what you think.

It will have to be pruned and you will have to be careful about where the curtains come. Three vigorous and swift acts: pretty, delicate, and tender.

Yours affectionately . . .

[1] *I.e.*, at Torre del Lago, where he was not far from the Tyrrhenian Sea.—TRANSLATOR.
[2] Teatro dei Filodrammatici in Florence.—TRANSLATOR.

167

To Giuseppe Adami

Torre del Lago

Dear Adami,

I have sent you *Mollie*. The name is unsuitable. We must find another. Read it and sketch out a scenario. I shall be in Milan (just passing through) within a few days, and so I don't suggest your coming here. That will be for later, when and if. . . .
Good-bye and kindest regards.
(Don't speak of our scheme to anybody.)

168

To Giuseppe Adami

Torre del Lago
November 2, 1913

Dear Adami,

And so you have read and discovered Dickens and Company? And how is *Mollie* or *Molly*? Are you thinking about her? If you have nothing urgent to do there why don't you take a run over to Torre? If you do, what with Dickens and Co. and *Molly* we shall arrive at something.
It will give me great pleasure if you will come.
Affectionately yours . . .

169

To Tito Ricordi

> *Milan*
> *April 11, 1914*

Dear Tito,

   Good-bye. Good wishes for Easter. I am just setting out. I heard *Gli Zoccoletti*[1] yesterday. Adami's version is excellent—delicate and sensitive. It will need touches here and there, some strengthening, and so forth, but the whole effect left me really pleased.

> Ever yours . . .

170

To Giuseppe Adami

> *Torre del Lago*
> *November, 1914*

Dear Adami,

   Let's go! Wire to Emanuel to ask the dates nearest to the 14th. Before the 14th is better, because then I could be in Berlin on the 17th for my conductor's *première* and be present, after countless invitations, at a performance of *Manon.* I am now waiting to hear dates, and am packing my bag. We can meet at Turin after midnight, at one, I think, when the Express *de luxe* arrives,

[1] The libretto adapted from Ouida's *Two Little Wooden Shoes.*—TRANS-LATOR.

leaving Pisa at six in the evening (I believe, I shall enquire). I don't know whether it would be best for you to take a return ticket. I shall be going to Berlin, and you, I suppose, certainly not. Arrange for yourself. If you are not coming to Berlin take a return Milan-London, *via* Modane.

Affectionately yours . . .

171

To Giuseppe Adami

Torre del Lago
Thursday, April 29, 1915

Dear Adamino,

I have been back for two days and have begun work again. And when do you think of coming here for a bit? It is very nice here. How is the stomach? And the new house? And your family? I must speak with you about *Gli Zoccoletti*. Come soon. Tonio is here too just now, so we shall make the *trinum perfectum*.

Yours affectionately . . .

172

To Giuseppe Adami

> *Torre del Lago*
> *Tuesday*

Dear Adami,

In that precious Dutch book with the water colours there is a delicious little picture. It is just right for the last act—before the procession of flowers. It shows six old men seated on mounds of earth and little green clumps, six worthless, idle, useless old fellows, gossiping about the tragedy that has happened, and telling over the story of the little *bébée* who was born among the water lilies and died in the pond. They are recounting the tale of her sorrow and the agony of her return, the tale which the children will tell again in another poem in the legend of the *intermezzo*. These old men could make a picturesque and characteristic group, because I think that the women will all be in the procession which will follow the poor little corpse.

I wanted to say this to you before you wrote the little scene which will precede the last.

XI
Turandot

PUCCINI'S last opera, *Turandot*, was produced at the Scala on the evening of April 25, 1926.

It was an unforgettable night of mingled triumph and grief, described in the *Corriere della Sera* by Gaetano Cesari, who wrote:

How extraordinary is the power of evocation possessed by music which bears in itself the clear imprint of the composer's personality! Last night at the Scala Puccini was with us. He was with the great public who had admired and applauded him in the days of his most splendid triumphs. He was in the theatre which, if it gave him some pain in the days of his striving, was not less generous with praise and homage, as on that occasion in particular when its genial conductor brought before the public again, in new beauty and freshness, the composer's most vigorous opera.[1]

Until last night's performance Puccini's vision of the tale of *Turandot* had remained a secret. Like the beautiful and cruel princess whose name it bears, the opera had kept closed within itself its own enigma. The mysterious prince, although perhaps foreseeing his success, had awaited his trial like the other, hiding in his heart the trepidation which he must have felt. Yet a few beats from the firm baton of Toscanini sufficed to bring before the great assembly the living spirit of the sweet singer of Manon, of Mimi, and of Butterfly. The exotic colour and the unfamiliar setting lessened in no degree the sense of his presence felt from the first notes of *Turandot*.

[1] The reference is to Toscanini's production of *Manon Lescaut* on the thirtieth anniversary of its first performance.—TRANSLATOR.

The artist was among us yesterday with the sadness of his own tragedy. "If I do not succeed in finishing the opera," he had said one day, with a presentiment of his approaching death, "some one will come to the front of the stage and say, 'Puccini composed as far as this, then he died.' " The opera stopped yesterday at the point where Puccini had had to leave it. Thus *Turandot* ran its course like a living symbol of the life of its creator: a brief story, interrupted by a pause which is of eternity. The performance, punctuated by frequent applause, ended with a moment of silence, when the little, mangled body of Liù disappeared behind the scenes followed by the procession of the mourning populace, and a shrill E flat from the piccolo seemed to tell once more of the fleeting soul and of the far-off and forever impenetrable mystery, to which alike great passions and obscure loves like little Liù's come at last and are lost. Then, from where he stood as conductor, Toscanini announced in a low voice full of emotion that at that point Puccini had left the composition of the opera. And the curtain was slowly lowered on *Turandot*.

This moment of intense emotion will not be repeated. For at the second performance the opera will be given with the addition of the last duet and the short final scene of which Puccini had merely outlined the music.

What searching and what torment went to the creation of *Turandot* are clear to see in the letters of Puccini which follow! He had loved no opera so much as this one, born of an ardent desire to break away from the drama of common life and to try those untrodden ways which for long had drawn his hungry and restless spirit.

In September, 1924—just two months, alas, before his death—Giacomo Puccini sent the joyful announcement to his collaborators: "Toscanini has just left me. We are in perfect agreement. I have said yes for the Scala."

Four years of unremitting labour were crowned by this joyful communication; four years during which *Turandot* had matured and grown, after infinite searching, with all the time an unsatisfied thirst and a continuous torment in the mind of the composer without a subject: "I am burning to start work, but I have no libretto and am in torment," he wrote. But, as always happened before he made his final choice, innumerable ideas and projects were shattered, dashed against the rocks of that marvellous theatrical vision and that infallible instinct which counted among the supreme qualities of the great musician.

It was truly a desperate problem. Although Adami and Simoni had had a kind of official commission to make a libretto and had with confidence and good-will devoted themselves to the quest, they were for long unsuccessful. The composer was accordingly idle, and his vivid letters throbbed with impatience and pleading.

Puccini had come to Milan on one of those flying visits of his, with his heart fixed, from the moment of his arrival, on returning again to his "lair," as he called it, among his pines. And it was on that afternoon in the spring of 1920, just a few hours before his departure, that Simoni in a last, desperate attempt, said: "What about Gozzi? Shall we ransack Gozzi? A fairy-tale? A kind of synthesis, if possible, of his other most typical tales? Something . . . I don't know . . . something fantastic and unreal, but interpreted with human feeling and presented in modern colours? . . ."

The spark had fallen on fuel that waited to burst into

sudden leaping and joyful flames. And from the smoke and sparks what should spring out clear and scintillating but the name of the cruel Princess? And amid a saraband of Chinese dancers, and a scent of exotic perfumes and powders of bygone days, there advanced, imperious and regal, proud and fascinating, enigmatic and irresistible, Turandot the beautiful.

Puccini took home with him the volume containing Schiller's version of Gozzi's tale, and a few days later he had decided definitely to make it his subject. But from the simple structure of the old story it was essential to make the hidden source leap out fresh and living. Had not Carlo Gozzi, in fact, written *Turandot* as a reply to the accusation that he "depended entirely on the power of mechanism and phantasmagoria," and as an effort to free himself from the heroic and magical and to attain more nearly to the simple and poetical atmosphere of the fairy-tale? And if others before him had borrowed from that old Persian tale, from Shakespeare, who in *The Merchant of Venice* substituted for Turandot's three riddles the three caskets of Portia, to Molière who finds his inspiration for *La Princesse d'Elide* in the character of the proud Chinese princess who rebels against love, it was obvious that there was a good dramatic basis in the story, for one who knew how to profit thereby.

To the Court of Pekin in long caravans from every part of the world come princely suitors for the hand of Turandot. The cruel Princess rejects them all, propounding to them three almost insoluble riddles with death as the penalty for failure. The example of the many who have died is of no avail, such is the beauty and fascination of the unattainable. This Turandot almost to the last inflexible and indomitable, was to come to life once more in the midst of a hotch-potch of strange and barbarous incidents, customs, and ceremonies, through which peeps travestied the honest conscience of the Venetian mask.

Puccini showered advice upon his librettists. His suggestions always shed new lights; and a touch, an indication, was often sufficient to reveal fresh aspects or give original lines to the story, enriching it not only in its general conception, but also in detail, in spirit, and in scenic effect. Thus, Gozzi and Schiller forgotten, there grew up little by little a new *Turandot*, vibrant, moving, and real, as Puccini had conceived and desired it.

These letters record all the different phases through which the opera passed before it assumed its final form, and bear witness to the fervour with which Puccini worked. They discredit the many tales of the ease with which he wrote his music and attained his good fortune. They show instead how great was his theatrical genius, with what anxious research, with what ardour, and with what tremulous anxiety he approached his art, and, above all, how he lived from day to day and from hour to hour in the anguish and joy that belonged to his high calling.

Sometimes he was a prey to infinite discouragement. But if by chance he felt that his gloom was affecting his collaborators he would fight down his own melancholy and call them back to courage with no uncertain voice.

As one by one the difficulties were overcome and the work proceeded, his faith increased. It was when the opera was all but finished that his illness began to loom large in the minds of all, although no one would believe that Puccini might die.

In his last letters we find a shudder of despair, and at the same time, trembling underneath it, a pulse of hope for his life and his art.

What am I to say to you? . . . I am having a horrible time. This trouble in my throat is giving me no peace, although the torment is more mental than physical. I am going to Brussels to consult a well-known specialist. Will it be treatment? . . . Or sentence of death? I cannot go on like this any longer. And then there's *Turandot*. The lines are good—exactly what were needed and as I had imagined them. So the duet is ready. As soon as I get back I shall set to work again. . . .

But he did not come back!

He had taken with him to the fatal clinic his manuscript of the *finale* of the opera, exactly thirty-six pages of composition and notes. He hoped still to be able to work, even there. He hoped to be able to finish his opera, a task which, as he himself said, would have taken at the most three weeks.

But Fate decreed that Giacomo Puccini should close his eyes forever at the same moment as his little Liù, the last of his creatures, and with the same subdued and sorrowful song of beauty and tender poetry.

(The following letters were all addressed to Giuseppe Adami.)

173

> *Torre del Lago*
> *October 23, 1919*

Dear Adami,

Well, have you and Simoni come to grips? Put all your strength into it, all the resources of your hearts and heads, and create for me something which will make the world weep. They say that emotionalism is a sign of weakness, but I like to be weak! To the *strong*, so-called, I leave the triumphs that fade; for us those that endure!

> Yours affectionately . . .

174

> *Torre del Lago*
> *December 17, 1919*

Dear Adamino,

I have your telegram. It is all right. But I am going away today and shall not be back for three days. I think that I shall not be able to come to Milan for the present. Have you got it all ready? But is it in outline only, or already in verse? I intend going to my Tower in the Maremma after Christmas. I must have an inaugural ceremony. I have everything ready. Will you come? Or will you send the manuscript here first that I may get some idea of it? I should say that this last idea

The First of the Thirty-six Sheets on which were
Outlined the "Turandot" Duet and Finale

of ours is the best. If it is gold it will glitter to my eyes too. What do you think of it? Answer at once, so that I may find the letter here on my return. You know that the post is slow of foot.

Poor Illica! Another friend gone! One after another, a sad catalogue that goes on lengthening pitilessly! We have to resign ourselves, but one chafes all the same. What a life!

All good wishes to you, to Signora Amalia, to Nené, and to your baby girl—and good wishes, too, that your work may be, as we Tuscans say, of God's own making.

Regards and best wishes to Renato, too.

Affectionately yours . . .

175

Torre della Tagliata[1]
Wednesday Night, February 3, 1920

Dear Adami,

Here I am. I am thinking of you and Renato and of the subject you are going to give me. Don't forsake me. I am in a hurry too. I am enjoying being here. It is wonderful just now when the moon is full.

Affectionately yours . . .

[1] Puccini's retreat in the Maremma, the "inauguration ceremony" of which is mentioned in the preceding letter.—TRANSLATOR.

176

Sunday

Karadà,[1]

I don't feel like coming to Milan. I am sending you the volume of Schiller. We shall discuss the matter by letter, and anyhow the business of the moment is to adapt the story. Choose a style for it, make it interesting, pad it, stuff it out, and squeeze it down again. It is impossible as it is. But worked at and well masticated, it should turn out a kind of Sir Robber, a sort of *taking* gentleman. Hurrah! I am getting some scenic material from Germany. I have a book of Reinhardt's already, but there is little of *Turandot* in it. I shall get some old Chinese music too, and descriptions and drawings of different instruments which we shall put on the stage (not in the orchestra). But at the same time you two Venetians must give an interesting and varied modern form to that relative of yours, Gozzi. Don't talk about it too much, but if you succeed (and you must) you will see what a beautiful and original thing it will be, and how *prenante* (and this last is essential). Your imagination, together with all those sumptuous fancies of the old author, must inevitably lead you to something great and good!

Do your utmost.

Yours affectionately . . .

---

[1] Puccini writes *Karadà*—an Oriental effect in keeping with their eastern subject—for *Caro Adami.*

177

Monday Night

Dear Adami,
 The postcard is pretty, but it is not Reinhardt's *Turandot*. I do not feel like coming to Milan just now. It is better that we see each other later on—you must prepare an outline. Do not hurry it. You must ponder it well and fill it out with details and embellishments.
 Make Gozzi's *Turandot* your basis, but on that you must rear another figure; I mean—I can't explain! From our imaginations (and we shall need them) there must arise so much that is beautiful and attractive and gracious as to make our story a *bouquet* of success. Do not make too much use of the stock characters of the Venetian drama—these are to be the clowns and philosophers that here and there throw in a jest or an opinion (well chosen, as also the moment for it), but they must not be the type that thrust themselves forward continually or demand too much attention. Good-night, dear Adami. I am leaving tomorrow for Torre del Lago.
 Kind regards to Renato.
      Affectionately yours . . .

178

Torre del Lago
Friday Evening

Dear Adami,

Immediately on the receipt of your express letter today I wired to you on a first impulse, advising the exclusion of the masks. But I do not wish this impulse of mine to influence you and your intelligence. It is just possible that by retaining them *with discretion* we should have an Italian element which, into the midst of so much Chinese mannerism—because that is what it is—would introduce a touch of our life and, above all, of sincerity. The keen observation of Pantaloon and Co. would bring us back to the reality of our lives. In short, do a little of what Shakespeare often does, when he brings in three or four extraneous types who drink, use bad language, and speak ill of the King. I have seen this done in *The Tempest*, among the Elves and Ariel and Caliban.

But these masks could possibly also spoil the opera. Suppose you were to find a Chinese element to enrich the drama and relieve the artificiality of it? So I come to the conclusion that for the moment I am adding neither salt nor pepper. I leave it to you and may the good God give you inspiration!

Keep well.

Yours affectionately . . .

'*17th, 11.20 P.M.*

Dear Adamino,
  If I touch the piano my hands get covered with dust. My desk is piled up with letters—there isn't a trace of music. Music? Useless if I have no libretto. I have the great weakness of being able to write only when my puppet executioners are moving on the scene. If only I could be a purely symphonic writer! I should then at least cheat time . . . and my public. But that was not for *me.* I was born so many years ago—oh, so many, too many, almost a century . . . and Almighty God touched me with His little finger and said: "Write for the theatre—mind, only for the theatre." And I have obeyed the supreme command. Had He marked me out for some other task perhaps I should not be, as now, without material. O you, who say you are working while you are really doing something quite different—films, plays, poetry, articles—and never think, as you ought to think, of one who has the earth under his feet and yet feels the ground receding from him every hour and every day as if a landslip would swallow him up! I get such nice encouraging letters, but if, instead of these, one act were to arrive of our glittering Princess, don't you think it would be better? You would give me back my calm and my confidence, and the dust would not settle on my piano any more, so much banging would I do, and my desk would have its brave array of scoring

sheets again. O you of the city, think to more purpose of one who is waiting in the country! I need not only the first act, but the third also, since then Act II would be finished. And *La Rondine?* When are you bringing it to me? It is urgent because it has forty theatres waiting.

Affectionate regards to you and Renato.

180

May 15, 1920

Dear Adamino,

Turandot! Act I—very good! I like the *mise en scène* too. The three masks are very successful. I am not quite sure about the effectiveness of the close, but I may be wrong. The truth is that it is a good act and well laid out. What will the second act be like? Shall we need the third? Or will the action be exhausted in the second? Go ahead with it, using all your imagination and resourcefulness, and the opera will be not only original but *moving.* And it is on this last that I lay most stress, and this we must achieve. Good Beppino and Renato! Thank you! I go to London on Tuesday for eight or ten days. I beg you to get on with the work, so that I may as soon as possible get an idea of the whole thing.

Affectionately yours . . .

181

Torre del Lago
July 18, 1920

Dear Adami,
Your packet to hand. At first sight it seems
to me good, except for some criticisms which I might
make in both the second and third acts. In the third—I
had imagined a different *dénouement*—I had thought
that her capitulation would be more *prenante*, and I
should have liked her to burst into expressions of love
coram populo—but excessively, violently, shamelessly,
like a bomb exploding.

We must meet. Will Renato come to Bagni di Lucca?
Will you? You will understand that I don't want to
come and roast in Milan, but it would be convenient (I
mean it is urgent) to meet as soon as possible. We've got
our canvas, a large one, and an original and perhaps
unique work. But it needs some alterations, which we
shall devise when we meet to discuss it.

All my affectionate regards to you and Renato.

182

Torre del Lago
September 25, 1920

Dear Adamino,
I've had a letter from you at last! I have written to you—I have written to Simoni. I have told Val-

carenghi to see you—I wrote to him the other day to the same effect. Let this prove to you, therefore, with what impatience I am awaiting Acts I, II, and III of *Turandot*. I have filled a good number of music sheets with jottings and indications of ideas, harmonies, and movements. I have sent for books. I have received one which I am sending to you but which *I want back again* because there is some music at the end which may be useful to me. In short, don't go to sleep, my dear poets, I am tired of idleness.

I am leaving for Vienna in a week or so, for *La Rondine* and perhaps *Il Trittico*, both in the same month, October. *La Rondine* is first, and *Il Trittico* is before the 10th of October. Will you come to Vienna?

Kindest greetings.

Yours affectionately . . .

183

Vienna
October 20, 1920

Dear Adamino,

God willing, I am leaving here on Tuesday night. I can't stand it any more—such frightful cold I have never felt in my life. Two more days and I am back in my lair again. Send me those feathers that you have been plucking from our bird of ill-omen.[1] But let your alterations be few—few and effective and necessary—

---

[1] *La Rondine (The Swallow)*, which had undergone further alterations.

otherwise I leave it as it is in the first edition and good-bye to it.

Berté has requests for thirty theatres. So you will come either to Torre or to La Tagliata, because I am going to the Maremma as soon as possible—*i.e.*, about the 20th of November.

And is *Turandot* sleeping? The more I think of it, the more it seems to me the sort of subject that one wants nowadays and that suits me perfectly. But it must have a good comic element and the right kind of sentiment.

It seems that they are producing the play[1] in Berlin towards Christmas or later. We three shall go together. I am already savouring the pleasure of that little jaunt.

All good wishes to you and Simoni.

184

Torre del Lago
November 10, 1920

Dear Adamino,

I have found your letter. I reached Torre after a journey of three days. I missed my connections and had to sleep at Venice and then at Bologna.

So you think that I was made happy and am happy now as a result of the welcome I had at Vienna? I have carried about with me on all my journeys a large bundle of melancholy. I have no reason for it, but so I am made,

[1] Schiller's *Turandot.*—TRANSLATOR.

and so too are made all men who feel and are not fortified by stupidity.

I am afraid that *Turandot* will never be finished. It is
impossible to work like this. When the fever abates it
ends by disappearing, and without fever there is no creation; because emotional art is a kind of malady, an exceptional state of mind, over-excitation of every fibre and
every atom of one's being, and so on *ad aeternum*. I am
going to the Maremma towards the end of the month
to become still more brutish. Will you come there, or
do you prefer to come here first? It depends on you
and the work you have done. And what about Simoni?
Now that the thrushes have gone south will he get
to work? Is he still on his high horse, I wonder? I
hope not, because for me the libretto is nothing to trifle
with. It is not a question of finishing it. It is a question
of giving life that will endure to a thing which must be
alive before it can be born, and so on till we make a
masterpiece. Shall I have the strength to second you?
Who can tell? Shall I be tired, discouraged, weighed
down by years and spiritual torment, and by my never-
ceasing discontent? Who can tell? Work as if you were
working for a young man of thirty, and I shall do my
best; and if I do not succeed it will be my fault!

Affectionately yours,

185

Torre della Tagliata
December 24, 1920

Dear Adami,
    I beg you not to forget the cruel Princess. (Don't you think that that golden rose act is rather gentle?) You must hurry with the alterations of *La Rondine.* I hope that you have had a good journey and wish you a Merry Christmas.
Brilliant sunshine today.
Greetings and think a little of this voluntary prisoner. Greetings also to my dear Renato.

Affectionately yours . . .

186

Torre del Lago
March 30, 1921

Dear Adamino,
    I have written to Simoni for the *finale.* How are you getting on with Act III? I shall be coming to Milan soon. On Saturday perhaps I am going to Rome for two or three days—and from there I shall come straight to Milan.
    Here at Torre it is dull and almost unpleasant. Everything has its day, even Torre del Lago! The place has lost

all its *cachet*. The morning siren is now supreme.[1] It is disgusting!

I go to and fro between here and Viareggio, getting a little shooting, and looking after arrangements for the new house which seems to be approaching completion, and so my days pass. They are giving *Manon* at Rome. As I am going to Rome I'd like to hear a rehearsal.

Pay special attention to Liù in Act III. You will have to adopt an irregular metre. I have the music ready; it has a Chinese flavour, but I shall have to make some changes. Affectionate greetings to you and Renato and good-bye till I see you.

187

Torre del Lago
April 30, 1921

Dear Adamino,

Turandot is going well; I feel that I am on the highroad. I am at the masks, and in a little while I come to the riddles! I think I have made great strides. What about Act II? And III? For God's sake, don't wear me out with waiting.

Regards to you all.

[1] The siren belonging to some peat-workings which were begun a few yards from the composer's villa.

Torre del Lago
Thursday

Dear Adamino,

As long as I see the bills unchanged at the Olympia[1] the sun shines for me, and may it continue long to shine! I have written to Renato to hurry him up.

When you turn your feet towards Rome I'll take it as a slight if you don't stop at the Lake, where friendly faces and tender green asparagus await you. *Turandot* is groaning and travailing, but pregnant with music. O sticky-windy-bovine animals—which being interpreted is collaborators[2]—think of Act III. You must draw upon all your resources of sentiment and emotion. You must move your hearers at the end—and you will know how to do that! Not much rhetoric!—and let the coming of love be as a shining meteor while the people shout in ecstasy, their taut nerves vibrating to the pervading influence like the deep-toned strings of a violoncello.

I, for my part, will find phrases worthy of your golden numbers. I shall suck my brain with a crystal tube to fill my pentagram[3] with phosphorus. And all for you, for us, for the people, for the world!

Salvatote, bards and prophets!

[1] Puccini is referring to *Parigi*, a play in five acts by Giuseppe Adami, which had a particularly long run at the Olympia Theatre in Milan.—TRANSLATOR.

[2] An instance of the kind of puzzle which frequently adorned Puccini's speech with intimates. He wrote here, *attaccaticci* ("sticky")—*vento* ("wind")—*bestie bovine* ("bovine animals"), with the explanation *colla* ("glue")—*bora* ("north wind")—*tori* ("bulls"), the whole forming the Italian word *collaboratori*. —TRANSLATOR.

[3] The five-lined stave.—TRANSLATOR.

189

> *Torre del Lago*
> *June 7, 1921*

Dear Adamino,

Congratulations for Turin. Your laurels are blossoming now.

And Viareggio in summer? You are still of that mind? Or are you going to the Great Bard.[1]

I am working like a Roman slave. It is terribly difficult, but I am getting on. I am finishing the masks[2] (frightfully good). But I have already done the music for the ghosts and the two songs for Calaf and Liù.

> Yours affectionately . . .

190

> *Torre del Lago*
> *Sunday, June 12, 1921*

Dear Adami,

Am I utterly forsaken by my beloved brethren in *Turandot*? Not a word—after so many promises, so much communion! I need the second act in a day or two! And I am needing, too, to feel myself loved a little and, like a faithful dog, to wag my tail. But as far as you two are concerned, I have a long face and my tail is drooping. You should have come here—first you, then

---

[1] D'Annunzio.—TRANSLATOR.
[2] The scene of Ping, Pang, and Pong in Act I.—TRANSLATOR.

Renato. I have written too much to you already. I shall write no more, I swear it. But it is the *Princess* who needs you. For her sake, at least, give me a sign that I am not yet a bit of old iron fit to be flung on the scrap-heap.

Yours affectionately . . .

191

Torre del Lago
June 20, 1921

Dear Adamino,

I am in a devilishly bad mood. Perhaps I am not well. I am completely stranded. I need encouragement from some one who understands me. Why don't you come here for some days? I should like to let you hear what I have done and judge whether it is work to tear up or to keep. God knows! Sometimes I think it all good, and at other times just the opposite. I am at the riddles now, and I am not getting on. I think I am out of sorts these two days. I am dining at Viareggio tonight. It will be, if not a distraction, at least a break in the eternal monotony of this *now* unbearable Torre del Lago. Bring me your third act. I shall need it in a little while. Is Renato coming? And when?

I think I am developing neurasthenia. What about Ricordi? If you will only come—both of you—you will give a little happiness to your . . .

192

Torre del Lago
Sunday

Dear Adamino,

I am not in doubt at all. I think that *Turandot* in two acts is right. The action begins at sunset and ends with the following dawn. The second act is at night, the first rays of dawn appearing at the end. So we come to an end with the rosy dawn and the sunrise.

Why not have an original scene after Calaf's cry, "I have lost her"? A scene *à la* Shakespeare[1] in front of a special curtain in which they would sing—standing still if you like—a hymn to the risen victory? Or else a dance, and add an epilogue with Liù, slaves, and Turandot? And then the final scene? In short, I do not think we should delay long after the riddles. Delay here means weakening the opera. Even the incidents of the second act are not important apart from the duet and the torture. The importance lies in the threat of death to the Prince and the suggestion of flight which precedes it. I shall come to Viggiù, and we will discuss it.

Consider this well, clearing your mind of the ideas which you already have and of what you have already done, with regard to the second and third acts.

Affectionately yours . . .

[1] Puccini is thinking not of Shakespeare's usage, but of the drop curtain by which the modern theatre deals with his frequent changes of scene.—TRANS-LATOR.

193

Torre del Lago
September 14, 1921

Dear Adamino,

I have sent Renato a plan of the second act. Enter Turandot, nervous after the ordeal of the riddles. A short scene ending with the threat: "Let none sleep in Pekin." *Aria* for tenor. After that do away with the banquet and have instead a scene in which the three masks dominate the action. With bribes of riches, wine, women, they beg and beseech Calaf to speak. "No, for so I lose Turandot." Anxious proposals of flight. "No, for I lose Turandot." Then daggers drawn and threats to his life. Conference of dignitaries, rapid conspiracy, and attack on Calaf. Enter Turandot; flight. Duet, shorter —then torture (and this should be quicker, too) to "I have lost her." Exit Turandot, in great agitation. Liù remains to speak to Turandot. Darkness—change of scene. Room in yellow and rose—scene of Turandot and slaves —the cloak. Pangs of jealousy. Darkness. Then the last scene, imposing, in white and rose: *Love!* What do you think? If you like it I shall come to Simoni's, and in a few days we shall make a great act.

Affectionately . . .

194

September 21, 1921

Dear Adamino,
 I am in despair as black as night.
We must meet. I have written to Renato. I shall come
to Viggiù, and you shall be there too. We shall put in
some work, and let us hope that we shall be able to arrange things to our satisfaction. I am still in favour of an
imposing and varied second act which will also be the
last. *Act I*, Sunset; *Act II*, Dawn. One thing is certain:
we must inspire the whole thing with life. As it stands
it is absolutely impossible, all wrong, I am convinced. It
has no pulse of life, no lightness of movement. I know
that the subject is not easily convincing, but just for this
reason you must be more sparing of words and try to
make the incidents clear and brilliant to the eye rather
than to the ear and, above all, give them variety. Every
scene must have a beautiful beginning and a more beautiful ending. I could go on like this, but I have said
enough. When shall I be able to come, and when shall
I be able to work?
                    Affectionately . . .

November 1, 1921

Dear Adamino,

I am in bed with a slight fever. Has Clausetti told you of the new piece, the monologue of the baritone which I should like to insert instead of that soliloquy on the river at the end of *Il Tabarro*? I want him to begin with some short isolated phrase when the lovers are passing. Then a sob, when "silence" is sounded (trumpet from within). Then he peeps into the cabin: "She isn't sleeping. . . . I know that she cannot sleep. . . ." And after that a few despairing lyrical lines. In short, I want something direct, and telling, emotional, original, and not long. That monologue is too academic altogether, and weakens the end of the drama.

All my affectionate greetings. What of Renato? And *Turandot*?

P.S. Did you get a note from me indicating what I wanted about the passage in *Tabarro*?

I want a poem which will allow some variety of movement in the music. And I want it to finish with a *muoio disperato*[1] in four or six rhythmic lines, rhymed, and suited, above all, to a musical flight which I hope to find with the help of your words. That river monologue chills and chokes the close.

How I hate these three operas! You cannot ever imag-

---

[1] "I die despairing"—Cavaradossi's cry in *Tosca*.—TRANSLATOR.

ine it. At Bologna they seemed to me as long as a trans-atlantic cable; but it wasn't my fault. But I should like to remove that philosophic solo and insert in its stead a human outburst, a sob or a curse from the poor bargeman of the Seine. And so, dear author of *Manon*,[1] finish the little *Cloak* and that quickly.

Greetings to Signora Amalia, to Nené, and your little girl.

196

Bologna
Monday

Dear Adamino,

I am sorry that you are not coming. The première will be postponed because the scenery which was sent from Naples has not yet arrived. So Renato is back in Italy? Good.

Turandot gives me no peace. I think of it continually, and I think that perhaps we are on the wrong track in Act II. I think that the duet is the kernel of the whole act. And the duet in its present form doesn't seem to me to be what is wanted. Therefore I should like to suggest a remedy. In the duet I think that we can work up to a high pitch of emotion. And to do so I think that Calaf must *kiss* Turandot and reveal to the icy Princess how great is his love. After he has kissed her, with a kiss of some—long—seconds, he must say, "Nothing matters

---

[1] Giuseppe Adami is the author of *Manon*, a play in five acts on the subject of Prévost's novel.—TRANSLATOR.

now. I am ready even to die," and he whispers his name to her lips. Here you could have a scene which should be the pendant to the grisly opening of the act with its "Let no one sleep in Pekin." The masks and perhaps the officials and slaves who were lurking behind have heard the name and shout it out. The shout is repeated and passed on, and Turandot is compromised. Then in the third act when everything is ready, with executioner, etc., as in Act I, she says (to the surprise of everyone), "His name I do not know." In short, I think that this duet enriches the subject considerably and raises it to an emotional interest which we have not now attained. What do you think of it? Tell Simoni.

My life is a torture because I fail to see in this opera all the throbbing life and power which are necessary in a work for the theatre if it is to endure and hold.

All my affectionate greetings.

197

November 8, 1921

Dear Adami,

Why—why "do you love me no longer"?[1] Why? Am I fallen—dethroned? Then there is no place left for me but Madeira.[2] I have been ill. I am still rather low in spirits. I sink lower than ever when I get no letters

[1] *Non m'ami più?* Manon's words in the scene with Des Grieux in *Manon Lescaut*, Act II.—TRANSLATOR.

[2] The place of exile of Charles Habsburg, last Emperor of Austria, sent to Madeira in October, 1921.—TRANSLATOR.

from you. As for Simoni, his silence is such that it *buries* me altogether! I am in black despair about *Turandot.* I wrote that to you before. Perhaps it is the fact that I have returned to the idea of two acts that makes you so taciturn?[1] It could also be a challenge. But you two will not take it up, and you withdraw into the shadows of indifference. It is not thus that I should be treated. If you have so often expressed your faith in me and have always considered me a good judge of matters theatrical you ought to listen to me and not simply hide your heads under your wings. Your wings must be spread and your heads high—we shall win! I have said, and I repeat, that Act II as it stands is a great mistake. After a first act which is so beautiful, so rich and spectacular, and above all so well balanced and convincing, it is absolutely necessary to have a second act which will be the quintessence of effectiveness, and the individual incidents must be clear and telling. I consider the duet as the *clou*—but it must contain some great, audacious, and unexpected element and not simply leave things as they were in the beginning, interrupting them only with cries from within of people arriving.

I could write a book on this subject. But it is late. I am going to bed—cursing a little; for I am far from happy!

Yours affectionately . . .

---

[1] There is a play here on the word *tacito*, "silent." Puccini wrote *Tacito*, which is the name of a play by Giuseppe Adami.—TRANSLATOR.

Rome
November 11, 1921

Dear Adami,

I am grieved by your letter. Do you think
that I am doing this because I am weary of the subject?
God knows it isn't that! But I think that with a more convincing and effective second act our bark will ride safely
into harbour.

I feel that this act as it is does not convince me and
cannot convince the listener. There are certain laws which
a theatrical composition must observe: it must interest,
surprise, stir, or move to laughter. Our act must interest
and surprise. Leave Gozzi alone for a bit and work with
your own logic and imagination. Perhaps you could develop it differently, more daringly? One never knows. By
myself I cannot find the way. But if you attack it with
a will, I think that you will arrive at something good.
I am the one of the three of us who least of all should
give up. I have already written the music for Act I, and,
good or bad, the act is there. Therefore don't tell me
that you see *Turandot* fading away! That would be a
shame! I do not know, but it seems to me that all your
will to work with me is dying out. And I am grieved
about it. You have said to me so often, "If it is not right
we shall do it again, but we must finish it." You will
have received a letter of mine from Torre del Lago in
which I discussed the duet and was even returning to the

[283]

idea of one single act, closely packed with incident, to finish the opera. I am still of this mind, although the general opinion is that two acts are not enough for an evening's performance. What does it matter, if the opera turns out more convincing and conclusive in this form?

We must meet. This is absolutely necessary. I shall stay here for four or five days.

Love.

199

Torre del Lago
November 17, 1921

Dear Adami,

I received your telegram in Rome the day before yesterday.

You tell me that you are working. Good! But how? In what form? On what idea? Have you paid attention to what I have written to you? We must meet. I wrote to Renato proposing to him to come here. It was also a possible fulfilment of his desire for shooting and for me a great pleasure, especially as there are woodcock on the lake just now. But *ancune réponse*!

I shall have to return to Rome about the 25th for the perusal of the operas (twenty-five!) presented for the competition. Time is pressing, and I think continually of the infinite *(inachevée) Turandot*. That first act—I am sure of it—is good. Why don't you get on? We must get it finished, and successfully. I have some ideas, extrava-

gant perhaps, but not to be despised. The duet! the duet!
It is the meeting-point of all that is decisive, vivid, and
dramatic in the piece. Tell Renato to make up his mind,
and write me some news that will comfort me.

Yours affectionately . . .

What about those four lines for *Il Tabarro*? Aren't
you going to do them? Tell me.

200

> [*Rome*]
> *December 21, 1921*

Dear Adami and Simoni,

I received at last your Pan-Tuscan letter from
the Maremma which you like less on closer acquaintance.
Here I am in Rome. The day after tomorrow I shall return to Viareggio for Christmas, and immediately after
I go to Milan for the New Year. I feel how much you
are seeing eye to eye—in fact, how much we three, etc.,
etc. *Optime*. And now to work!

I need the trio scene for the *finale* of Act I. And with
regard to the new Act I, if you find that you can expand
it in some directions, do so. This to make it less rapid.

And for the first scene of Act II, consider the daughter
of the sky, high up beside the Emperor's throne, beseech-
ing and praying that she be not thrown into the stranger's
arms.

I am thinking of the twenty-five operas which I ought

[285]

to be judging, but which I am not judging because I am left alone. Mascagni is at Pisa conducting *Marat*.

Toscanini has withdrawn for numerous reasons of his own. Bossi has a son competing, so he has made off too. Cilèa is in Naples. There remain, therefore, d'Atri, who has given proof of musical judgment, but . . . and Rosadi, who hums the masses of my eighteenth-century ancestor. *Ergo* I am not skinning this cat!

Good-bye. Love to you both. Be good fellows and work for me.

Affectionately yours . . .

201

Viareggio
December 26, 1921

Dear Adamino,

Yesterday, in the new house,[1] I played the first act of *Turandot* through again after so long a time. I liked it, and Consolo too, who was there, said things which comforted me. If only you could bring down the curtain after the three masks have finished their pleadings and almost exhausted their powers of persuasion! The two—the old father and the slave girl—must say all they can to persuade him, the three masks adding their prayers; then after Calaf's hymns (phrased like the trio in *Faust*), finish with the beating of the great gong. But

---

[1] Puccini had moved to Viareggio from his once beloved Torre del Lago which the opening of peat-works and a noisy siren had completely spoiled for him.—TRANSLATOR.

I am preaching to the converted. It is needless to say more—you already know all about it. I am writing now to fill my paper—but I am in a fever to have some work to do, and while I have not this work on my table I am in torment.

But we shall see each other soon.

To close this random letter I send you all best wishes for the Christmas season and the coming New Year.

Affectionately yours . . .

202

Viareggio
May 2, 1922

Dear Adami,

I had written in despair yesterday to Simoni about your appalling silence. Thank you for your comforting letter today. All right. When? You say soon. But I have heard the same thing so often! I have been passing through a crisis with regard to my music. Yes—because I am utterly disgusted with everything. But perhaps I felt more disgust at the lucubrations of the music of today. (No allusion to Ricordi's paper.[1])

Turandot is going ahead, if only as far as the orchestra is concerned. I think it is going well. But, of course, I can't be sure.

What are you doing now? I *must* have something original, something which is the product *entirely* of your

[1] *Musica d'oggi (Music of Today)* is the name of a musical review published by Ricordi.—TRANSLATOR.

young brain, something delicate and moving—not too much psychology—but sympathetic understanding of human grief or again a touch of gay, fresh laughter. But I think that you are more likely to be convincing with the emotional element. And it is this that makes a work succeed and endure. Otherwise it may succeed, but it is a victory which is soon forgotten. And now, my panegyric ended, I am looking forward to your coming with the third act ready for our adjustments.

All good wishes.

203

Viareggio
July 9, 1922

Dear Adamino,

I am expecting you every day. I have no news at present from Ricordi.

I have reread Act III. I find much in it that is good. *Much*—but we shall have to make cuts—*many*—and the duet too, good at the beginning and in some of the rest, must, however, be touched up in the concluding section. I have some ideas. I am in favour of uniting the first and second parts, but in rather a different way. I should like the icy demeanour of Turandot to melt in the course of the duet, or, in other words, I want a love passage before they appear *coram populo*—and I want them to walk together towards her father's throne in the attitude of lovers and raise the cry of love while the crowd looks on

[288]

in amazement. She says, "I do not know his name," and he, "Love has conquered. . . ." And the whole ends in ecstasy and jubilation and the glory of the sunlight. Get rid of the Mandarin and the Emperor. The *finale* should follow on from the duet without a break, and the whole thing be swifter. What do you think? Will Renato approve? The work is a small matter for you. It is just a question of some new stanzas instead of those which you have already done. Come soon.

Love to you and Renato.

204

Viareggio
October 30, 1922

Dear Adamino,

Let us hope that the melody which you rightly demand will come to me, fresh and poignant. Without this there is no music. I am working, but I have so much before me to do! I am appalled too when I think of the burden of years that I carry. But—forward without trembling or fear! Send the stanzas, especially those for the *aria*. Has Simoni returned? And what about the thrushes? Did he get my postcard? Is he coming for the coot-shooting? Now that the *Corriere* is suppressed he has less work to do: I am waiting for him.

What do you think of Mussolini? I hope he will prove to be the man we need. Good luck to him if he will cleanse and give a little peace to our country!

I am glad that you are working. There is no better medicine than work for making one's existence less miserable.

I wish you great happiness.

205

Viareggio
Thursday

Dear Adamino,
I am hard at work again. I wrote you that the middle stanzas, the new ones, would be better condensed into one. The rest is all right. I am now finishing Act I at last, and I think that I have made a powerful ending. I have had no letter from you.

Are you remembering our idea of an opera on eighteenth-century Venice? I am still of the same mind and ready to start. It is frightfully dull here. It is raining. There was nothing to shoot today.

See if you can do anything with the lines:

> Trattieni quel pazzo furente;
> Su, portalo via!
> Su, un ultimo sforzo.[1]

After that I am writing (for want of words) "Hold him back and carry him off," and *vice versa*. But they can't both carry him off and hold him back.

Then Liù says her laconic "Signore, Signore," and so on like that. How on earth am I to make these people

---

[1] "Hold back that raging madman; quick, carry him off! Quick, a last effort."

sing? Timur too has hardly any words. I don't care what
metre you use, but I beseech you to make them say something.

I pray you again, with clasped hands, to send me four
lines for the masks, the same for Timur and also for Liù.
Make this last effort for Act I.

Thank you and may God reward you.

Affectionately yours . . .

Your idea for eighteenth-century Venice is excellent.
But is there an element of sorrow in it? Let there be at
least one tragic scene. Good luck to you!

206

November 3, 1922

Dear Adamino,

I am up now, but not at all well. The fever
has just left me. Let us hope that I shall soon be better.
I am so sad! and discouraged too. *Turandot* is there with
the first act finished, and there isn't a ray to pierce the
gloom which shrouds the rest. Perhaps it is wrapped for
ever in impenetrable darkness. I have the feeling that I
shall have to put this work on one side. We are on the
wrong track for the rest of the opera. I think the second
and third acts are a great mistake as we have envisaged
them. I am coming back, therefore, to the idea of two
acts, and getting to the end now in one other act. The

basis of the act must be the *duet*. Let this be as fantastic as possible, even if you should exaggerate. In the course of this *grand duet*, as the icy demeanour of Turandot gradually melts, the scene, which may be an enclosed place, changes slowly into a spacious setting enriched with every fantastic adornment of flowers and marble tracery, where the crowd and the Emperor with his Court, in all the pomp of an important occasion, are waiting to welcome Turandot's cry of love. I think that Liù must be sacrificed to some sorrow, but I don't see how to do this unless we make her die under torture. And why not? Her death could help to soften the heart of the Princess. . . . I am tossed on a sea of uncertainty. This subject is causing me tremendous anxiety of spirit. I wish that both you and Renato would come here! We could talk it over and perhaps save the whole thing. If we go on as we are doing, *requiescat Turandot!* Write. If you care for me and still wish me to work with you don't abandon me like this.

Affectionately yours . . .

207

Viareggio
November 11, 1922

Dear Adamino,

Here I am among the pines. The verses were not awaiting me as you promised. I am very anxious to finish Act I, because I have to go to Rome to judge the competition, and I should like to send the act to Ricordi before I go.

So I shall expect a letter from you. I saw Brunelleschi in Paris. He has made various costume sketches for *Turandot*. These I think you must see, because Brunelleschi has taste and should certainly not be ignored. For the scenery we must find some one else, but there is time for that. I spoke to him about the Venetian subject too. The idea attracted him very much. And there he will be the very man we need. What is Simoni doing? I have written several letters to him, but he makes no sign. What's the matter?

All good wishes from
Yours affectionately . . .

208

Viareggio
December 11, 1922

Dear Adamino,

I am rejoiced at the successful production of *Piccola Felicità*. How quietly you have done it! I knew nothing about it, and thought at first that it was the one we always spoke of as Galli's.[1]

Are you pleased? Best wishes for a good run.

I am coming to Milan in two or three days because I want to hear Pizzetti's opera, and *Manon* is going on immediately after.

[1] A play which had been projected by Giuseppe Adami for the actress Dina Galli.—TRANSLATOR.

I have no good news about *Turandot*. I am beginning to be worried about my laziness! Can I have had enough of China because I have composed one whole act and nearly finished the second? I am certainly failing to write anything else that is good. I am also old! Of that there is no doubt.

If I had found the sort of subject I was looking for, and am still hoping to find, I should have it staged by now. But this Chinese world! I shall certainly come to a decision of some sort in Milan. Perhaps I shall return the money to Ricordi and cancel the contract.

I should by this time have had the sketch of the Venetian opera, but so far there is no sign of it. Renato said that he would go ahead with it, and it was to be ready at the end of November. Do you remember? Anyhow, that was the arrangement.

I have tried again and again to write the music for the introductory scene of Act II and cannot.[1] I don't feel comfortable in China.

I am longing to see you. We must see much of each other; lots of dinners out!

Many kisses and hugs to dear little Doretta and warmest greetings to all the other coadamites.

[1] Act II, Scene I—the scene outside the curtain of the three masked figures, Ping, Pang, and Pong.—TRANSLATOR.

209

> *Milan*
> *March 6, 1923*

My dear Adamino,

No! no! no! *Turandot* no! I have received part of Act III. It is quite impossible. Perhaps—and maybe there's no perhaps—I too am no longer possible! But about this Act III there is no doubt at all.

I am not quite at the stage of crying, *Muoio disperato*, but very nearly.

I wonder if you could take it and make something out of it with the help of the old Act III? Is it possible? And shall I be able to do my part? I am very, very much afraid! Can we meet? Would you come to Torre with me? I hardly dare to hope.

Dear little Adami, I am a poor unhappy man, discouraged, old, abject, nothing! What am I to do? I don't know. I'll go to bed and sleep to escape the torture of thinking.

Good-night!

210

> *Viareggio*
> *March 12, 1923*

My dear Adamino,

Here I am—in a house of mourning.[1] I am alone. I am cursing *Turandot*! I want something tender,

[1] One of his sisters had died.—TRANSLATOR.

simple, clear, and—*ours*. If we can't find it, I'm giving up altogether!

Here sunshine and green growth outside, but in my heart blackness.

211

Viareggio
March 12, 1923

Dear Adami,

Thank you for the telegram. I have had a miserable time here alone. Now I am attacking Ping and Co. But I cannot find the right way. I wrote to you yesterday about what I wanted. What does Renato say about it? My regards to him.

212

[Viareggio]
March 25, 1923

Adamino, three letters, three appeals, three fragments of my heart; and no answer. I am working— I don't say full steam ahead, but have got started again, and God grant me good going!

I may need that wretched Act III at any minute. *Turandot* is proving a frightful bore to me, so we can imagine what it will be to the public. Are you coming or not? It's fine to be here, now that winter has gone and spring has come.

How is Simoni? Greetings to you both.

213

Viareggio
April 14, 1923

Dear Adamino,

Thank you for your letter. I have been ill in bed with an abscess in the mouth and fever, etc. Now I am better. I am waiting to hear from Vienna. But it is certain that I shall not be going till about the 20th. You ask about my work. Slow but good. Turandot's song is nearly finished, but what a labour it has been! Some change will be necessary, however, in the words. This song should not be at all bad, sung while she stands high above the stage at the top of the flight of steps. I am getting on with the trio of the masks too. This scene is very difficult and of the greatest importance, as it has no scenery and is almost purely traditional. And so amid the discouragements and the small and short-lived joys which accompany such work, *Turandot* is advancing, with slow steps, but sure.

I have written to nobody. I should have replied to you long ago. Forgive me and make my excuses to Renato.

Kindest regards to all your household. Come soon, and we shall settle everything.

Yours . . .

214

[*Viareggio*]
April 17, 1923

Dear Adamino,

I am not going to Vienna till the beginning of May. Could you therefore come here now? We could settle everything and you could also correct or alter some of your lines to suit the music, etc. Come. It will be such a pleasure to see you again. And don't forget the closing duet for which I am still waiting!

Affectionate regards to you all.

215

Viareggio
April 19, 1923

Dear Adamino,

Our letters have crossed. You will have received mine. There is time before I go to Vienna. If you come now we shall settle everything in a very short time. And if we had that duet, too . . .

I am suffering torments, but my work is progressing, although slowly.

Come—come! I await news of your arrival. Make Renato hurry up and finish. All good wishes to him.

Greetings to you all.

216

Vienna
Thursday [*May, 1923*]

Dear Adamino,
 In haste: arrived safely. Cool today, but very
warm journey.
 There is talk of *Manon* for September. They are giving
Capelli Bianchi in a few days. Eisenschitz wanted to give
you a pleasant surprise. If Jeritza accepts they will do
Manon. If not I shall return to my work. But I shall stay
here a little while for the festivities which they have prepared for me. They treat me here as if I were the Kaiser
or the Crown Prince. Living is enormously dear. My bed-
room and sitting-room cost 500,000 crowns a day. I am
well. My thoughts are on the lovely *Turandot,* lovely in
her newest attire, thanks to the great *tailleur* Adamino.
And talking of beauty, last night at the Opera, in Strauss's
Legend of Joseph there was an *ensemble* of the feminine
nude that would have turned the head of a St Francis.
Good-bye. Greetings to you all from all of us.

217

Viareggio
June 28, 1923

Dear Adamino,
 It is true that I am working, but not exactly
feverishly. Act III, however, is well begun with the voices

[299]

from within, and the famous *romanza* is finished at last. But I have taken a few liberties with the lines. I shall look into this afterwards with you, most able arranger and originator, man of just judgment. (Thank you!) (Not at all!)

At Varazze the day before yesterday I bought a motorboat that does over twenty-five miles an hour. It is the boat that won the races at Monte Carlo, and I shall have it in ten days. If you come we shall have some cruises and sail away into the far mists.

Elvira and I are here, the two *ancêtres*, like two old family portraits frowning from time to time at the cobwebs which tickle us. We sleep, eat, read the *Corriere*, and with a note or two in the evening the old composer keeps himself alive. Well? It would be a crime if you did not come to Viareggio!

Affectionately yours . . .

218

[Viareggio]
September 5, 1923

Dear Adamino,

Don't forget your promise to come here. It is quiet now, and you will be able to work in peace. Bring work with you and you will pass your time profitably. You will hear *La Fanciulla*, too, accompanied by all the usual kindly but boring festivities.

I am looking forward to your coming. *Turandot* is going ahead.

Greetings to Signora Amalia, to your little girl, and to Nené.

219

Viareggio
November 12, 1923

Dear Adamino,
　　　　Thanks for your letter. I rejoice in your success as heartily as if it were my own.

I am accomplishing nothing or next to nothing. Poor, neglected *Turandot*! Now that I have at last settled down to write a bar or two, I find that I have no lines for the death of Liù. The music is all there; it is a case now of writing words for music which is already made. It is only an outline, of course; it is impossible to develop the sad little scene satisfactorily until I get the words. If you will only come soon, I cannot tell you what joy it will give me. I need some seven-syllable lines to add to Liù's song. Shall I show you roughly what I mean? Here it is:

> Tu che di gel sei cinta
> da tanta fiamma vinta
> l'amerai anche tu.
> Prima di questa aurora,

(This line can be repeated, because it is effective.) Here you want a seven-syllable line, then another (they must be *very moving*). Then,

> io chiudo stanca gli occhi
> perchè egli vinca ancora;

[301]

io chiudo stanca gli occhi
per non vederlo più.[1]

220

December 17, 1923

Dear Adamino,

I have waited for your work in vain. In the meantime I have started to orchestrate Act II. I need the duet urgently. Try to strengthen it a bit. Keep the motives which we have decided upon and which are the essential ones, but if you can find some new elements to make it more interesting, so much the better. Then I beg you to think about the grand *finale*, in the metre of the tenor's *aria* for the final phrase, as we decided upon it.

I am in your hands, and I beseech you both with all my heart to make haste.

Poor Gallignani! What a tragic end!

Affectionate regards to you all.

[1] "Thou who with ice art girded,
Vanquished by so much fire,
Wilt love him, even thou.
Before this dawn awakens.
I close my weary eyes
That victory again be his;
I close my weary eyes,
Never to see him more."

221

> *Viareggio*
> *December 22, 1923*

Dear Adamino,

Milan has whirled you into its vortex and made you forget your *maestro*, who is still waiting for work. I wrote to you, and I write again, begging you to jog Renato. I have tried to hurry him up, and I have written to him again now.

What are you doing? Tell me about your plans and what you are writing. I am writing for the orchestra at present to save time, but I am desperately anxious to finish.

All good wishes.

222

> *Viareggio*
> *January 19, 1924*

Dear Adamino,

Please write me a stanza for the serenade[1]— one for the middle, in rhymed decasyllables like the others, *"Non v'è in Cina per nostra fortuna,"* a nice appealing little stanza. Thank you.

I am at the duet, and haven't got the words!

[1] End of Act II, Scene I. Ping, Pang, and Pong imagine themselves singing this serenade to the royal pair if ever Turandot should yield to a suitor's love.— TRANSLATOR.

I am sad and melancholy—discontented with everything, even *Turandot*! I am longing to be free of it. What
about yourself? What are you doing? Any new projects
afoot?

Write to me—I am always so pleased to get your letters.
Love to you all.

223

                                        Viareggio
                                        January 22, 1924

Dear Adamino,

            I have written to you for the stanza: I should
like it to have some assonances that would give it a
Chinese flavour. It must be sung *pp* in a subdued nasal
tone. It should come after the third stanza.

Something like this:

> *Canticchiamo pian piano* sommessi
> nell'uscir siam prudenti in giardin.
> *Se inciampiamo* nei sassi sconnessi
> disturbiamo il felice Calaf![2]

[2] "Let us hymn them in low, soft voices;
    In the garden let's tiptoe and creep.
    If we stumble on stones that are loosened,
    We shall waken the blissful Caláf!"

The lines which Adami supplied after this pattern were:
"*Nei giardini sussurran le rose*
e tintinnan campanule d'or,
si sospiran parole amorose
di rugiada s'imperlano i fior!"

("In the gardens the roses are whispering;
There are tinklings of golden bells,
And words of lovers sighing
And pearly dew on the flowers.")—TRANSLATOR.

The conception here is not good; neither is the imitation of Chinese syllables, but it gives you the idea of what I want.

224

Viareggio
Wednesday, or rather Thursday

Dear Adamino,

Thank you for your kind letter. I want just one other alteration (don't send me to the devil!) in those stanzas. I want the two middle ones made into *one* —it's a question of shortening.

It has been raining here for two days. I don't mind it. I keep my fire burning, but only for decorative purposes, as it is certainly not cold. There is still nothing from Paris.

Tomorrow at last the painters are coming for the new room.

I am cutting down twelve pines round the house so that we may have more air and to satisfy Elvira, who thinks that they cause damp. It breaks my heart to do it.

Hardly any sport at present. I have done two pages of *Turandot* today. I have sent off the final cry in the *Fanciulla* duet.

Yours affectionately . . .

225

Viareggio
January 23, 1924

Dear Adamino,

I should suggest that you come here at once,
and we shall fix everything up finally. We have the first,
second, and third versions to work on, and from these
three we shall construct the great duet. Between us, understanding each other as we do, and with such a quick
worker as you are, we shall soon produce the final version. I should like to return to the idea of internal voices
to illustrate psychological moments. I am certainly not
coming to Milan just now. I cannot leave my work on
Act III, which I shall begin to orchestrate today or tomorrow, and in Milan I am incapable of writing a single
note. Hence I await your telegram announcing the
Adamistic sacrifice, for which I tender my apologies and
crave your pardon.

Kindest regards to you all.

226

Viareggio
January 27, 1924

Dear Adamino,

No more news from anybody. Renato wired
me in New Year week, "In two days you will have

everything." And you? Why are you silent? I saw some news of you and your affairs in the *Corriere*. I stick to my table all day and every day. I am orchestrating. And I have so much to do still. I hardly ever go out. It does me good to read the letters of those who are dear to me, and you are silent!

Affectionately yours . . .

227

Viareggio
February 11, 1924

Dear Adamino,

Very good. I am pleased. And now you'll get on with something new. I have almost finished the orchestration of Act II, and I can assure you that it is going to be beautiful. Shall I be proved wrong, I wonder? You never know nowadays! I see triumphs accorded to hideous things that have neither feeling nor originality. . . . Well, well, we shall see. Try to extort the duet from Renato, then come here, and we shall settle everything.

Monte Carlo
Thursday

Dear Adamino,

Thank you for the lines, which are good. There is just one word which will not do: "I shall *shout* my love," because it occurs on a low note. But that is easy to change. Hour by hour and minute by minute I think of *Turandot*, and all the music I have written up to now seems a jest in comparison and pleases me no more. Is it a good sign? I think so.

My kindest regards to Renato. I send you golden spurs to speed you in the sacred race which we are running.

The rehearsals here are going well. I have seen nothing of them yet, as I wanted everybody there, so as to correct from a musical point of view. I shall see tomorrow at the full rehearsal. I am told that Gunsbourg has upset everything. The man amuses me! I am letting him do what he likes—especially as by now there is nothing else to do.

I too am homesick for you and the collaboration which is so precious and so delightful to me.

Kind regards to Renato and yourself.

229

May 19, 1924

Dear Adamino,

      On Friday at five Chini will take the sketches for the new scenery to Ricordi's. I think that now we are on the right track. I have made some suggestions about the garden, and we have still to choose the final scene, for which there is a choice of two. I have made suggestions too about the flight of steps. Go and look at it and decide, suggest alterations, etc. The lines have not yet come, and I am waiting! Kindest regards.

230

Viareggio
May 31, 1924

Dear Adamino,

      Simoni has sent me the duet in a prose version. He has introduced some embellishments and some slightly different ideas which I think are good. It remains now to put it into verse. As far as the action is concerned our plan remains unchanged, with the name performing the same function as before. So now we must make a metrical version and try to keep the rhythm of the existing version, particularly at *mio fiore mattutino*[1] and at the end, because, as you are aware, the music is already in existence—not yet elaborated, but the *idea* is the one

[1] "My flower of morning."

which you know. I have told Renato to look you up and arrange all this. And it seems to me no great matter, considering your fluency and ability. Kindest regards to you and Simoni. I am leaving here for Salso in ten days. Perform a miracle and send me the duet as quickly as possible to the Hôtel des Thermes.

Affectionately yours . . .

231

Viareggio
July 4, 1924

My dear Adamino,

I am bored. I must get this *Turandot* finished. Please send me the verses—I shall take the work up again, and it will do me good. Idleness does not suit me. Try to send me the *final version*, including the lines for the priests at the end of the march for the Persian prince —the "Hymn of Confucius." I have the score here and will put them in. See that you give me a good *finale* in the metre given.

Kindest regards. I am eager for your news. Why don't you come here for a few days?

Yours . . .

232

> *Viareggio*
> *September 1, 1924*

Dear Adamino,

I am starting to write again today. I have been passing through tremendous crises—with regard to my health as well as other things. The trouble in my throat that has been worrying me since March was beginning to appear serious. I am feeling better now, and have, moreover, the assurance that it is rheumatic in origin and that with treatment I shall be cured. But I have had some very black days. That is why I wrote to nobody, not even to you, which is saying everything!!

Clausetti came yesterday and I said yes for the Scala. I wonder if I was wise?

I shall start again now the work interrupted six months ago! And I hope soon to see the end of this blessed princess.

At the moment my horizon is clearer in every direction. Kindest regards. Why don't you come here for a little?

233

> *September 7, 1924*

Dear Adami,

Toscanini has just gone. We are in perfect agreement, and I breathe at last. So the weight is lifted which has oppressed me since April. We discussed the duet, and he does not like it much. What is to be done? I don't know. Perhaps Toscanini will ask you and Simoni to come to Salso. I shall come too, and we shall see if it is possible to improve the situation. I see no light at all. I have already reduced myself to a state of stupidity over this duet. Speak to Renato too about it. We must find a way out; for I am at my last gasp. My regards to you and Renato. . . .

P.S. The little that I played to Toscanini seemed to make a good impression.

234

September 14, Evening

Dear Adamino,

Are you really coming here? I wish you would! There is much disagreement about our duet, and I am rather worried! What am I to do? I was hoping that you and I might have a meeting with Simoni and Toscanini at Salso, but up to the present I have received no summons. We must therefore settle the matter ourselves. I have some ideas in my mind for the duet. The beginning I shall not change unless something better is suggested. And so will you come? Kindest regards.

235

                                        Viareggio
                                        [*September, 1924*]

Dear Adamino,

     I have written to Renato. We must meet. If
you come here we shall fix things up. Bear in mind also
our first idea of introducing internal symbolic voices,
speaking of liberation for the love which is coming to
birth and helping and encouraging it.

     It must be a great duet. These two almost superhuman
beings descend through love to the level of mankind, and
this love must at the end take possession of the whole
stage in a great orchestral peroration. Well, then, make
an effort. Come!

                                        Yours . . .

236

                                        Viareggio
                                        October 8, 1924

Dear Adamino,

     At last I have received the lines from Simoni.
They are very beautiful, and they complete and justify
the duet.

     There is one word, *esile* ["slender"]—"like a flower"
—which must be changed. I beg you to look at the
libretto again, along with Renato and change the stage

directions and please try to make up your minds about the *mise en scène* for the trio in front of the curtain. For the staging keep in mind the pictorial ideas of Chini, following the lines of his work where you can. For the trio scene in front of the curtain you could introduce an openwork marble balustrade interrupted in the centre like this:

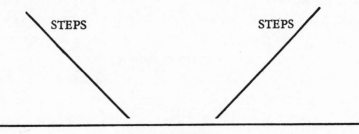

STEPS   STEPS

FOOTLIGHTS

And this could be retained also in the following scene with the flight of steps. On this balustrade the masked figures play their part, sitting or lounging on it, or astride it as the case may be. I am not explaining very well what I mean, but I know that in the *Ariadne* of Strauss at Vienna they did something of the same sort with the Italian masks;[1] only there the masks climbed up by two stairs from the orchestra. Perhaps that would hardly do at the Scala—so make the masks come in from descending steps at the sides. It is my opinion that we must invent something special for this trio scene. Discuss it with each other—and if you could also see Caramba ask his

---

[1] Harlequin and company, the familiar masked figures of Venetian comedy, enter incongruously into the scene of Ariadne forsaken on the island of Naxos, in Richard Strauss's opera composed to follow *Le Bourgeois Gentilhomme* of Molière.—TRANSLATOR.

advice. I am very sorry now not to have the collaboration of Caramba, but you know better than anyone how we were placed with regard to Brunelleschi.

I hope that Clausetti will make an effort to cancel that agreement, particularly as it is not impossible that Brunelleschi would withdraw, being terrified by the shortness of the time and the two hundred or more figure-sketches to be made. All the same, Brunelleschi too is an artist of great ability. It now becomes a question of sentiment, and both artists are precious elements in our collaboration. . . . Well! Meanwhile, go to Simoni, not to Viggiù, of course, but I expect that he will occasionally take a run down to Milan between two shoots. You will have to find out when he is making one of those flying visits, then get into touch with him and snatch an hour for our work.

Yours affectionately,

GIACOMO PUCCINI

Sonatore del Regno[1]

What are you doing just now? Work hard and believe in yourself.

[1] Puccini had recently been made a Senator of the Kingdom of Italy (*Senatore del Regno*). He alters his title here to *Sonatore* ("musician").—TRANSLATOR.

237

Viareggio
October 10, 1924

Dear Adamino,

Is it really true that I am not to work any more? Not to finish *Turandot*? There was so little still to do for the successful completion of the famous duet. Come, come, dear little Adami, do me this favour, make me the great effort of devoting two or three hours to me and send me the lines which I need. But do this little piece of work in such a way that it will be final and not have to be returned again. Don't disappoint me!

Affectionately yours . . .

238

Viareggio
October 22, 1924

Dear Adamino,

What am I to say to you? I am going through a terrible time. This trouble in my throat is giving me no rest, although the torment is more mental than physical. I am going to Brussels to consult a well-known specialist.[1] I am setting out very soon. I am waiting for a reply from Brussels and for Tonio's return from Milan. Will it be an operation? or medical treatment? or sentence of

---

[1] The trouble had been diagnosed as cancer, but Puccini himself had not been told this.—TRANSLATOR.

death? I cannot go on any longer like this. And then there's *Turandot*. Simoni's verses are good, and I think he has done just what was needed and what I had dreamed of. All the rest of Liù's appeal to Turandot was irrelevant, and I think your opinion is correct that the duet is now complete. Perhaps Turandot has too much to say in that passage. We shall see—when I get to work again on my return from Brussels.

Let us hope that I shall get over this!

Yours affectionately . . .

[The following letter was written on the day of Puccini's arrival, accompanied by his son Antonio, at the hospital in Brussels.]

239

> *Institut Chirurgical*
> *Avenue de la Couronne*
> *Bruxelles*

Dear Adamino,

Here I am ! Poor me !

They say that I shall have six weeks of it. You can imagine how pleased I am!

And *Turandot?*

Affectionately yours . . .

[The letter which follows was written two days before the fatal operation and was the last letter which Puccini wrote.]

[317]

240

Dear Adamino,

So far the treatment is not too bad. External applications. But on Monday God knows what they are going to do to me, in order to get at the epiglottis from underneath! They assure me that it will not be painful—and they say too that I shall be cured. Some days ago I had lost all hope of recovery. And what hours and days I have passed! I am prepared for anything.

Write to me sometimes.

Yours affectionately . . .

My regards to Signora Amalia. Elvira is in Milan.

After the operation the hopes of everyone revived. Carlo Clausetti, in fact, wrote the letter which follows:

Brussels
November 26, 1924

Dear Adami,

I am writing to you on my own account as well as for Tonio and Fosca.[1]

I shall summarise all the news for you thus: *Things are going better than anyone could have hoped. The doctors are now saying without any hesitation that Puccini will certainly recover.*

You will understand that no doctor would dare to make a pronouncement of this kind unless he were absolutely sure of being right. Doctor Ledoux, moreover, is not given to op-

[1] Fosca is a member of the firm of Ricordi.—TRANSLATOR.

Puccini's Last Letter (No. 240)

Written on the eve of the fatal operation in the
hospital at Brussels

timism, but is, on the contrary, somewhat rigid and reserved in character. During the days which preceded the operation his replies to the inquiries of the management of the Théâtre de la Monnaie were not particularly reassuring; but yesterday he sent a message to them of his own accord:

Puccini en sortira.[1]

Four days have now passed since the operation, and no complication has set in; we need therefore no longer fear that any will arise. The heart is in perfect order, and the lungs and bronchial tubes are functioning with the greatest regularity. The whole task is given over now to the radium which is to be his miraculous saviour. For it is of nothing less than a true and authentic miracle that we must speak, and but for the able doctors of Brussels our poor and illustrious friend would certainly have died.

As I write he is sleeping peacefully. He is a little nervous and anxious at times, but that almost gives us pleasure, for it shows that his vitality is returning.

We have now to exercise some calm and patience, because without doubt the treatment and convalescence will take a very long time—but we are all happy to wait, now that his recovery is certain.

On Sunday Doctor Ledoux will remove the needles, and thus the first—and most painful—phase of the treatment will be at an end.

I shall remain here until Monday or Tuesday at the latest. Then I am going straight to London, where I shall stay for a few days. I am breaking my journey at Paris on my way back, and will take a run over to Brussels, where I feel sure I shall have the joy of finding Puccini already far on the way to recovery.

I am sure I need not tell you that we have kept him informed

[1] "Puccini will pull through."

of the affection and concern with which you have followed his painful ordeal and that he appreciates it very much.

Please remember me very kindly to your wife and with all good wishes to yourself, I am,

Sincerely yours,
CARLO CLAUSETTI

Following immediately on this came the tragic telegram which, as with the merciless seal of destiny, closes these letters.

Brussels
November 28, 9 A.M.

Serious cardiac crisis supervened. Fear worst. All heart-broken.

CLAUSETTI

Puccini died at 11.30 A.M. on Saturday, November 29, 1924, in the Institut de la Couronne at Brussels.

Index

A

Abbot Nerici, 29
Abetone, 158, 180, 184
Acqui, 158
Adami, Giuseppe, 7, 8, 26, 80, 187, 192, 194, 198, 203, 208, 215, 217, 223, 244, 245, 246, 251, 256, 259, 273, 280, 282, 293, 295, 304, 316
Addio fiorito asil, 157
Adolphe, 140, 141
A Florentine Tragedy, 167, 236, 240
Aïda, 30
Alba, 162
Albina, 53
Alcindoro, 107
Alfano, 191
Amalia, Signora, 196, 210, 261, 280, 301, 318
Amato, 173, 174
Amedio of Savoy, 58
America, 56, 74, 141, 163, 164, 168, 173, 238
Angeleri, 33
Angeloni, Maestro, 31
Anima Allegra, 212, 229, 244, 246, 247
Antinori, Piero, 172
Antonio Foscarini, 28
Aphrodite, 164
Arcachon, 229, 248
Aretino, Pietro, 239
Aria of Cavaradossi, 117
Ariadne, 314
Assunta, 51
Auber, 32

B

Bagni di Lucca, 267
Baltimore, 162
Barasso, 99
Barrière d'Enfer, 89, 90, 91, 98
Bassi, 174
Bauvet, 110
Bayreuth, 36
Bazzini, 29, 32, 33, 34, 43, 62
Belasco, David, 138, 141, 169, 170, 172, 173, 174, 237
Belasco Theatre, 172
Bellincioni, 177
Bergamasco, Caprino, 30
Berlin, 24, 243, 251, 252, 269
Bernard, Tristan, 242, 243
Bernhardt, Sarah, 115
Bersezio, Carlo, 82
Berta, 83
Berté, 187, 269
Biraghi, 37
Blanc, Signor, 49, 77, 148
Boito, Arrigo, 30, 33, 36, 37
Bolcioni, 77
Bologna, 27, 28, 106, 142, 161, 189, 269, 280
    University of, 152
Bolzoni, 39
Bonze, the, 166
Boscolungo, 180
Borelli, 77
Bori, 79
Bossi, 61, 286
Boston, 162
Bottesini, 55
Bracco, 159

[321]

INDEX

INDEX

INDEX

[324]

INDEX

INDEX

M

[326]

INDEX

INDEX

[329]

INDEX

Index to Letters

* Puccini's Mother
† Puccini's Sister
‡ Puccini's younger Brother
§ Puccini's Sister
¶ Puccini's Sister